Gubernatorial Elections in Alabama
1863

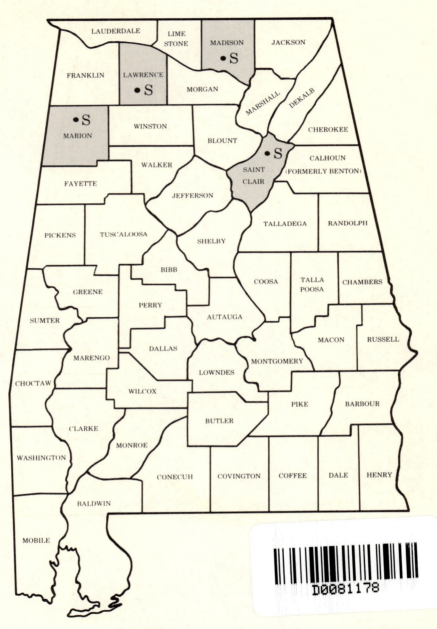

• S Shorter won four counties in 1863 (Madison, Marion, Lawrence, and St. Clair). All were in North Alabama in territory largely controlled by the Federals. The returns from Winston and Marshall in the same area were not counted by the legislature, which said they were "illegally reported." Watts's victory in 1863 was thus overwhelming.

This copy is dedicated to Dr
Ralph Draughon, my friend
and president of Auburn University
Mrs Draughon was one of his
greatest assets.

Malcolm C. McMillan
Oct 17, 1986

THE DISINTEGRATION
OF A CONFEDERATE STATE

MALCOLM C. M^CMILLAN

THE DISINTEGRATION OF A CONFEDERATE STATE

Three Governors and Alabama's Wartime Home Front, 1861–1865

MERCER
MUP

ISBN 0-86554-212-0

The paper used in this publication meets the minimum requirements
of American National Standard for Information Sciences—
Permanence of Paper for Printed Library Materials, ANSI Z39.48-1984.
∞™

Library of Congress Cataloging-in-Publication Data
McMillan, Malcolm C.
The disintegration of a confederate state.
Bibliography: p. 137.
Includes index.
1. Alabama—Politics and government—Civil War,
1861–1865. 2. Alabama—Governors. I. Title.
E551.M35   1986   976.1′041′0922   86-16346
ISBN 0-86554-212-0

CONTENTS

PREFACE

This study looks at the Civil War in Alabama through the office of the governor in order to ascertain whether conditions in Alabama, the birthplace and central state of the Confederacy, conformed to Charles W. Ramsdell's thesis that the "disintegration and collapse that took place behind the Confederate lines" was a major cause of the defeat of the Confederacy. In 1937 Ramsdell presented this thesis in the first of the Walter L. Fleming Lectures at Louisiana State University, but he did not document the lectures, which were published posthumously. Ramsdell listed the following generally assigned causes for the South's loss of the war: "the greater strength of the North—its much larger population and the heavier weight of its armies, its more extensive industrial development and material resources, its far greater financial strength, its possession of a navy with facilities for shipbuilding which enabled it both to blockade the southern ports and to keep northern waters open to the trade of the world and to thousands of immigrant recruits for the Union armies, and its ability through diplomatic pressure to forestall foreign recognition of the Confederate government." Yet, in preparing his lectures, Ramsdell noted that the usual explanations for Southern defeat or failure are insufficient because they overlook the disintegration and collapse that took place behind the Confederate lines. He argued that "the Confederacy had begun to crumble, or to break down *within,* long before the military situation appeared to be desperate."[1] Granting the validity of the causes already enumerated, this study

---

[1]Charles W. Ramsdell, *Behind the Lines in the Southern Confederacy,* ed. Wendell H. Stephenson (Baton Rouge, 1944) vi-vii, 1.

will focus on other internal problems that Ramsdell thought had been a major contributor to the South's defeat. Was the collapse of the home front in Alabama a major cause of the war's sudden end in the state? The evidence presented here argues that it was.

The Alabama home front viewed from the perspective of the state's three wartime governors presents the problems faced by the governors and their electorates at every stage of the war and examines Alabama's relationship with the Confederate government. This study could easily have focused on home-front problems and issues common to all three governors during the Civil War. However, a separate chapter is devoted to each governor so that significant materials on the background and administration of all three can be included. The chronological emphasis was chosen for its illustrative purposes. For example, it clearly shows that the war, as it affected the home front, underwent a steep decline during the second year of Shorter's term in office.

As a student of Alabama history, I was intrigued by the fact that Alabama's wartime governors were not given the opportunity to serve a second term, although Joseph E. Brown of Georgia remained in power from 1857 to 1865 and was twice reelected during the war. What made the difference? Presumably the people of Georgia faced the same problems and sacrifices. This work cannot possibly provide all the answers to this question, but I believe that it suggests many of them.

Another theme explores the idea that the abandonment of organized political parties in Alabama during the war greatly weakened its war effort. On the Confederate level, this theme was first presented by Eric McKitrick in his essay ''Party Politics and the Union and Confederate War Efforts.'' McKitrick argued that the suspension of organized political parties for the war paradoxically produced an opposition to Jefferson Davis that became unmanageable because without parties, the opposition became personal, factional, and sometimes irresponsible. He pointed out that during the war opposition to Lincoln in the North was channeled through the identifiable Democratic party, which necessarily handled its opposition more responsibly than individuals or factions could have done. Criticism of Lincoln could be answered by Republican party leaders if Lincoln wished to avoid the issue. The abandonment of political parties in the South, however, caused a loss of party support for Jefferson Davis and a resulting loss in the rewards of party support.[2] This study shows that on the state level, Alabama governors elected during the war were unable to lean on a strong political party for solace and support. Their electorates, too, were deprived of the educational processes that nominating conventions, party platforms, and open debate had offered in the past but which were now set aside in the name of unity. People were not exposed to the issues, did not know a candidate's stand, and, hence, had to vote a ballot that was at least partially blind. In effect, the issues were swept under the rug for each election. The abandonment of discussion and debate by the candidates inspired misgivings, frustrations, and a feeling of hopelessness in the electorate instead of unity and trust.

In developing these themes, I have highlighted the office of governor in one of the Confederate states. What did a Confederate governor do? What problems resulted from the war and how did the governor solve them? What were his thoughts on the war as he corresponded with Confederate authorities? Did the war leave a lasting imprint on the office and did the actions of Alabama's war governors affect the course of state politics and government after the war? I searched a thousand or more letters for each governor in the Alabama Department of Archives and History in Montgomery to find the answers to these questions.

It is my hope that this study will add to our knowledge and understanding of the Confederacy. I am convinced that it is a necessary chapter in the history of Alabama.

M.C.M.
Auburn, Alabama
August 1984

---

[2]Eric L. McKitrick, "Party Politics and the Union and Confederate War Efforts," in *The American Party Systems: Stages of Political Development*, ed. William Nisbet Chambers and Walter Dean Burnham (New York, 1967) 117-51.

INTRODUCTION

Alabama's politics and economy—and indeed every facet of its history during the Civil War—were inexorably connected with the state's geography and its land resources. The state was divided into distinct geographical regions and, before the railroads, these regions were practically isolated from each other. Nature did not connect northern and southern Alabama by water. Moreover, in the geological formation of the state, the foothills of the Appalachian Mountains divided the Tennessee Valley from the rest of the state. A plateau exists south of these mountains, but it soon runs into the Black Belt, where the limestone-based soil is especially adaptable to growing cotton. This soil is among the most fertile in the world. To the south of the Black Belt, the sandy coastal plain rolls gently to the Gulf. Central and southwestern Alabama are drained by a great river system (the Alabama and Tombigbee) that makes transportation and communication to Alabama's port of Mobile quite easy. In the antebellum period, central and southern Alabama faced Mobile. Southeastern Alabama, known as the "Wiregrass," was the exception to all this, and it remained sparsely settled before 1860. Like northern Alabama, it was a land of small farmers who barely made a living before there were commercial fertilizers to make the land productive and railroads to carry goods to market. The Wiregrass was "close kin" to northern Alabama in economic life and politics. As the cauldron of civil war reduced life to its essentials, southeastern and northern Alabama found themselves in agreement on the question of war and peace. When it became obvious that the protection of slavery was the basic issue in continuing the war, both sections realized that they had very little to win and much to lose. Neither section had many slaves, and they desperately wanted peace. The longer the war lasted, the stronger the opposition to it grew in both areas.

In the early antebellum period, northern Alabama's economic and cultural life was oriented toward the Tennessee River towns and, eventually, toward New Orleans as the waters of the Tennessee wound their way to the Gulf. After the completion of the Memphis and Charleston Railroad in the 1850s, Memphis—the largest city in Tennessee—became northern Alabama's metropolis. On the question of secession, northern Alabama was as interested in the choice Tennessee would make as in what central and south Alabama would do.

With the exception of some fertile land in the Tennessee and Coosa river valleys, northern Alabama was a land of poor white farmers. Politically, it was Democratic; its farms were small and without slaves. In many areas, the farmers eked out a mere existence on their poor soils.

On the other hand, the central and southwestern Alabama river country was a land of large plantations and slavery. In these areas, the Democratic and Whig parties had strength, with the Whigs often enjoying the most strength. Black Belt counties normally gave their votes to the Whigs, and the cities of Mobile, Montgomery, and Selma elected Whig mayors.

The two-party system came into being in Alabama during Andrew Jackson's presidency. Jackson's supporters were known as Democrats, while his opponents were known as Whigs. The Democratic party became the principal party of white farmers in northern Alabama, southeastern Alabama (the Wiregrass), and like regions of poor soil. The Whig party became the home of the planters, commission merchants, and others with wealth in the Black Belt and rich river-bottoms of the state.

Party lines became very fluid from 1850 until the beginning of the war. Both parties tended to divide into Union and States' Rights wings. In fact, both parties almost dissolved into the Union and States' Right parties during the debate on the Compromise of 1850. The Union party won the gubernatorial election of 1851 in Alabama—Alabama thus accepting the Compromise of 1850 as a basis for remaining in the Union.

However, as both parties in Alabama moved away from the compromise, the Democrats were able to reorganize and resume much of their old momentum. The Whigs, on the other hand, were unable to do so but kept their ideological hold on many of their former constituents. The American, or Know-Nothing party, which opposed Catholicism and the speedy naturalization of foreigners, came into being for a brief time in the middle fifties and filled the vacuum created by the organizational weakness of the Whigs. However, the American party soon disappeared because the main issue in the country was slavery and nativism could not take its place.

In 1854, the Kansas-Nebraska Bill brought the extension of slavery in the territories to the front as the main issue between the North and South. This issue further separated both old parties into States' Rights and Union wings. In the 1850s, Andrew Barry Moore, who was to become Alabama's first Civil War governor, belonged to the Union wing of the Democratic party until John Brown's raid and other developments forced him to become the secessionist governor of Alabama. The second of the wartime governors, John Gill Shorter, was in the States' Rights wing of the Democratic party and was a member of the so-called Eufaula Regency from 1850 until his election as governor in 1861. The last of Alabama's Civil War governors, Thomas H. Watts, was a Union Whig until he identified himself with the States' Rights group during the congressional campaign of his law partner, Thomas J. Judge, in 1857.

Meanwhile, in the North, the Americans, Whigs, and others were forged into the antislavery Republican party which elected Abraham Lincoln in 1860. The Democrats in the North remained strongly organized as the opposition party. Lincoln and the Northern governors enjoyed the benefits of the two-party system during the war, while Jefferson Davis and the Confederate governors were denied this main basis of the democratic process. Although opposition existed in Alabama and the rest of the South to secession and the war that followed, this opposition was not organized or identifiable as a party. Party conventions, platforms, and debate on the issues were buried for the war. Although its supporters claimed that the one-party system would unite Southerners for the war effort, it actually had the opposite effect—stifling democracy and all healthy expression of opinion. For instance, in the crucial election of 1863 in Alabama, the electorate was denied all information on which to cast an intelligent ballot.

Any consideration and evaluation of Alabama's three Civil War governors must take into account the fact that all of them came from the cotton-growing Black Belt of central and southern Alabama, a region that had emerged as the most influential in the state in the late antebellum period. Andrew Barry Moore of Perry County, John Gill Shorter of Barbour County, and Thomas Hill Watts of Montgomery County were all lawyer-planters of wealth who owned Black Belt plantations. Moore owned thirty-four slaves in 1860 and Watts, the largest slaveholder in the secession convention, owned 179. Shorter maintained ten slaves at his home in Eufaula, but most of his 100 slaves lived on his plantation across the Chattahoochee in Quitman County, Georgia.

Sectionalism, based on geographical and economic interests, had always existed between northern and southern Alabama, in part because of the mountains and the lack of transportation across them. Rife in the fifties, it was acute in the secession convention of 1861. ''Cooperationists'' of northern Alabama were virtually dragged out of the Union by ''immediatists'' to the south. The vote in the convention was sixty-one for immediate secession, and thirty-nine against. However, the vote of fifty-five to forty-six, by which the immediate secessionists organized the convention, reflected the true feeling of the delegates. After the vote, the immediatists then denied the cooperationists a referendum on the question of secession. These proceedings accentuated the existing sectionalism within the state. The April 1862 enemy occupation of Alabama, north of the Tennessee River, further divided the state. The long, hard, self-sacrificing war brought a political climate that virtually limited any governor to one term, in spite of a long-standing two-term tradition. Thomas Watts, the old Whig and Unionist who did not embrace the idea of immediate secession until after the election of Lincoln, would also have been limited to one term if the war had not ended when it did.

CHAPTER I

ANDREW BARRY MOORE:
Union Democrat
Turned Secessionist

Governor A. B. Moore had less than a year left of his second term in office when Alabama seceded on 11 January 1861—the fourth of the Southern states to do so. Though the Confederate States of America had not yet been formed and war was still three months away, Moore had already moved to prepare his state for war. Days before the secession convention voted to take Alabama out of the Union, he had ordered the seizure of federal military installations, including two forts on the Alabama coast. Such action suggests that Moore was one of those who ''breathed fire'' on the sectional issue—someone in sympathy with extremists like William L. Yancey. In fact, however, he had been a staunch supporter of the national Democratic party in Alabama and a strong voice for moderation until John Brown's raid on Harper's Ferry.

Born in Spartanburg District, South Carolina, 7 March 1807, the son of Captain Charles Moore (a Revolutionary War and War of 1812 soldier), he was reared on a South Carolina cotton plantation. Although none are specific, all accounts say that he received a good education. His state papers certainly indicate a man of superior intellect and education. Like many other South Carolina planters with depleted lands, Moore's father moved west, settling about 1823 at Marion in Perry County. Andrew was sixteen at the time and, perhaps because of his schooling, did not move to Marion until 1826. After teaching school for two years, he read law and began to practice in 1833. With the growth of agriculturally rich Perry County, Marion, its county seat, developed into an important educational and cultural center. Moore's law practice prospered, and in 1837 he married Mary Goree, the daughter of a local planter, and moved her to his plantation in the eastern part of the Marion District.[1]

Moore was elected to the state House of Representatives on the Democratic ticket in 1839 but was defeated in the William Henry Harrison Whig tide of 1840. He was reelected in 1842 and enthusiastically supported the main issue of the session, the white basis of apportionment, which counted only whites in drawing the boundaries of the state's congressional districts. Although the white basis of apportionment was of northern Alabama origin, Moore's support was not incongruent. He was a Democrat, and the substitution of the white basis for the Federal ratio gerrymandered the congressional districts against the Whigs. However, because of the strength of the Whigs in Perry County, his position required considerable courage. He defeated the Whigs of Perry in the election of 1843 and, in the following legislative session, was elected to the powerful post of speaker by the Democrats.[2] As speaker he worked with Governor Benjamin Fitzpatrick in the liquidation of the State Bank and its branches, which Moore called "so many cancers eating into the very vitals of the body politic."[3] Speaker in the two sessions which followed (1844 and 1845), he supported the twin amendments to the constitution permitting the designation of another site for the capital city and providing for biennial sessions. After the amendments were ratified and Montgomery was chosen as the capital,

---

[1]Thomas M. Owen, *History of Alabama and Dictionary of Alabama Biography*, 4 vols. (Chicago, 1921) 4:1222; Willis Brewer, *Alabama: Her History, Resources, War Record and Public Men* (Montgomery, 1872) 490-91; Obituary in Mobile *Daily Register*, 10 April 1873; Manuscript Census of Alabama, 1850, schedule 1, 739.

[2]William Garrett, *Reminiscences of Public Men in Alabama for Thirty Years* (Atlanta, 1872) 720-22.

[3]Quoted in William H. Brantley, *Banking in Alabama, 1816-1860*, 2 vols. (Birmingham, 1967) 2:237.

Moore as speaker made the last speech in the old hall of the House in Tuscaloosa.[4]

A contemporary described him as "about six feet in stature, stout and well built, with good features and florid complexion." In his dealings he was said to be "frank, cordial, moral, and full of public spirit," a man deserving of "the highest respect."[5] In 1843 a fellow legislator described him as "a clever fellow but scary, has a good opinion of himself and is on the fence between the Hunkers and the Chivalry" (the conservatives and states' righters).[6] Moore's ability to deal with rival factions in the Democratic party was his strong suit and the factor largely responsible for his serving as speaker for three years. After his legislative years ended, he remained active in the party, playing a moderating role against the secessionists until the impending election of Lincoln.

Moore resumed his law practice in 1846, but he was appointed to the circuit bench by Governor Henry W. Collier in 1851 and then elected and reelected until nominated for governor in 1857. Although he held no office between 1846 and 1851, he was politically active, helping to save the state for the Democratic party by 881 votes in the Cass-Taylor presidential election of 1848. A delegate to the Nashville Convention from the third congressional district, Moore counseled moderation in the crisis of 1850-1851, giving his support to Governor Collier, a moderate who supported the Compromise of 1850 in the gubernatorial election held the following year. In November 1850 Moore wrote Bolling Hall that ninety-nine percent of the people of Alabama favored some kind of resistance to the North, but that few would advocate secession.[7]

Moore received the Democratic nomination for governor in 1857, defeating four other candidates in a twenty-six-ballot contest. Rivalry was intense within the Democratic party because the weakness of the opposi-

---

[4]Ibid., 256.

[5]Brewer, *Alabama*, 491.

[6]Virginia Knapp, "William Phineas Browne: Business Man and Pioneer Mine Operator of Alabama," *Alabama Review* 3 (April 1950): 116.

[7]Quoted in Lewy Dorman, *Party Politics in Alabama from 1850 through 1860* (Wetumpka AL, 1935) 64; Clarence Denman, *The Secession Movement in Alabama* (Montgomery, 1933) 25; J. Mills Thornton III, *Politics and Power in a Slave Society: Alabama, 1800-1860* (Baton Rouge, 1978) 178.

tion made the Democratic candidate a certain winner. Moore was a moderate on the sectional issue. All of his opponents, except John E. Moore of Lauderdale County, were extremists. In the election that followed, Andrew Moore had no opposition because the Americans and Whigs were too weak to organize. Dissension within the party grew and, when Moore came up for reelection in 1859, William F. Samford, friend of William L. Yancey and fellow agitator, announced his "Independent Southern Rights" candidacy against the governor. He was supported by the extreme Southern rights section of the party while Moore had the support of the more conservative national Democrats, still in majority. Samford complained that the Southern cause had not received "the earnest, active, outspoken sympathy" from the governor that it deserved. Charging that Moore had betrayed the cause when he failed, according to legislative instruction, to call a convention to give the voters an opportunity to express an opinion regarding secession after the passage of the Kansas Conference Bill, he bitterly censured the governor. Moore replied that the resolution applied only to Congress's outright refusal to admit Kansas as a slave state. The governor was overwhelmingly reelected, by a ratio of more than two to one, indicating that the people still accepted the national Democratic party as the defender of Southern rights. They had rejected the attempt of Yancey and Samford to organize a separate Southern Democratic party. Moore and the other regulars were still looking to the national Democratic party to defeat the Republicans in 1860 and then *protect* the South.[8]

Moore would have been remembered mainly for his state welfare program if the Civil War had not overtaken him. The asylum for the insane at Tuscaloosa, in which he had a personal interest (his wife was a mental patient), and the school for the blind at Talladega were both built while he was governor. State support for education was also increased. Governor John Winston had opposed all state aid for internal improvements (1853-1857), but Moore moved cautiously in this direction, advocating state aid to supplement federal land grants for railroads in the 1850s. Moore was particularly interested in connecting southern Alabama with the Tennessee River and pressed for building the Alabama and Tennessee River Rail-

---

[8]Dorman, *Party Politics,* 137-38; Thornton, *Politics and Power,* 265-66, 360, 363-64.

road, which reached as far as Blue Mountain in Talladega County before the war prevented its completion.[9]

National issues began to dominate all others. Governor Moore, who had previously spoken softly on sectional issues, became genuinely alarmed after John Brown's raid at Harper's Ferry in October 1859. He devoted most of his second inaugural address, delivered in December of that year, to the rights of the South, an issue that he had not even mentioned in his previous message to the legislature. He felt that he had been deluded by the Kansas-Nebraska Act and the Dred Scott Decision into believing that peace was at hand, but now realized that he was wrong. "The measures and this decision, so far from arresting the progress of black Republicanism and giving peace and quiet to the country, were seized upon to influence and prejudice the public mind in the non-slaveholding states," he said. Moore told the people of Alabama that he placed his hopes in the Constitution of the United States, which guaranteed equal rights to all citizens. He continued to advise them to look to the national Democratic party for the enforcement of these rights.[10]

Upon the governor's recommendation, the legislature passed a Military Bill that provided for the organization of a volunteer corps in each county, appropriated $200,000 for defense, and established military scholarships for two young men from every county in the state to attend military schools. In turn, after graduation they were to come back to the counties to train other young men to be soldiers. Feeling that direct trade with Europe would help solve the alleged problem of the South's economic exploitation by the North, this same legislature passed an act to encourage such trade and instructed Governor Moore to appoint a commissioner to carry out the act. The governor appointed Francis S. Lyon of Demopolis.[11]

Although Moore was now thoroughly aroused, one of his moves showed that he was still a moderate Southern rights man seeking to avoid the issue

---

[9]"Albert B. Moore," *History of Alabama* (Tuscaloosa, 1934) 312-13; Ethel Armes, *The Story of Coal and Iron in Alabama* (Birmingham, 1910) 107-10. For U.S. land grants to railroads, see A. B. Moore Collection, Alabama Department of Archives and History, Montgomery (hereinafter cited as ADAH) 23 March, 21, 30 June, 15 November 1860.

[10]Second Inaugural Address, in Montgomery *Weekly Confederation*, 10 December 1859.

[11]Denman, *Secession*, 68, 76-77; *Acts of Seventh Biennial Session of the Alabama General Assembly, 1859-1860*, 14-16, 36-39.

of secession. During the legislative session of 1860, Governor William H. Gist of South Carolina sent him joint resolutions of the South Carolina legislature proposing a Southern convention to consult upon "secession from the Union." At the same time, the "fire-eaters" in the Alabama legislature were demanding resolutions providing for a state convention in the event of the election of a "Black Republican" as president. Governor Moore saw the Alabama resolutions as the lesser of two evils. As one scholar has written, "The governor, terrified at the thought of taking so unequivocal a stand, hit upon the pending [state] secession convention resolutions as a device for postponing decisive action on South Carolina's request."[12] This would put off the day of decision and, in the governor's words, "if [a Republican victory] does not occur, there will be no necessity for a convention."[13] The contingency resolutions passed the legislature with only two dissenting votes, and Governor Moore wrote Gist that Alabama favored a separate state convention, upon the contingency cited, and a Southern convention later.[14] In retrospect, we know that the governor only postponed the day of decision by a matter of months, but from Moore's viewpoint the Democratic party, which had held the nation together in the fifties, might do so again in 1860.

However, the party split at Charleston and other events soon convinced Moore of the likelihood of Lincoln's election, and the governor began to prepare for the worst. Pressure was already building, especially in northern Alabama, to rescind the contingency resolutions; others wanted the governor to act immediately in calling a state convention.[15]

On 16 October 1860, Moore wrote E. C. Bullock of Eufaula that Lincoln's victory now seemed assured and that he was asking his friends in the legal profession to review his conviction that since the electoral college officially elected the president, he should not call a convention until after

---

[12]Thornton, *Politics and Power*, 406.

[13]*Journal of Seventh Biennial Session of the Senate of the State of Alabama, 1859-60* (Montgomery, 1860) 127 (hereinafter cited as *Senate Journal*).

[14]A. B. Moore (hereinafter Moore) to W. H. Gist, 2 April 1860, Moore Collection, ADAH. Unless otherwise stated, all manuscript material on Alabama's Civil War governors is in ADAH.

[15]S. D. Cabaniss to Moore, 29 October 1860; Tuscumbia *North Alabamian*, 21 December 1860; "Albert B. Moore," *Alabama*, 412.

the electoral college met in December. Moore stated that he wished to be on sound legal ground so as not to give the submissionists an issue in the election for the convention or the convention itself. He added that the convention "should be convened at the earliest day the law will permit and it is my determination to do so." Bullock replied that he was in complete agreement with Moore's interpretation and that, in his opinion, this was "such construction as would be given them by the courts."[16]

After Lincoln's election, pressure began to build for the governor to announce his intentions. On 14 November he said that he would not issue a proclamation calling a convention until after the vote of the electoral college on 5 December but, unofficially, set the election for convention delegates on Christmas Eve. Those elected would gather in Montgomery the following 7 January. Thus, by announcing his plans, the governor added three weeks to a campaign which, for reasons of expediency, was too short.[17] Although Moore did not verbally take sides in the campaign between the "immediate secessionists" and the "cooperationists" that followed, the public had known since his second inaugural that the governor believed that the election of a Republican on an antislavery ticket was sufficient cause for immediate secession.

In the meantime, Governor Moore started taking action. To an extent, he undercut the cooperationists by giving them a lesson in cooperation. He sent sixteen commissioners to confer with the officials of other slaveholding states, ostensibly to consult, but actually to coordinate and urge secession. These commissioners were very carefully chosen. The brother of the governor of Mississippi was sent to that state, and native ties of birth and interest were nearly always key determining factors in the selection process. Commissioners between states were usual in all the cotton states, but Moore had strongly influenced this movement by his early initiative and emphasis on the need for coordination. This fact is well illustrated in the *Official Records,* where the correspondence between Moore and his commissioners composes more than ninety percent of the entries on that sub-

---

[16]Moore to E. C. Bullock, 16 October 1860; Bullock to Moore, 22 October 1860.

[17]See letter of citizens to Moore and Moore's letter to citizens in William R. Smith, *The History and Debates of the Convention of the People of Alabama, January, 1861* (Atlanta, 1861) 12-15 (hereinafter cited as Smith, *Debates*).

ject. The commissioners also kept Moore and the Alabama secession convention abreast of what was happening in the other Southern states.[18]

In the crisis atmosphere that prevailed after Lincoln's election and the secession of South Carolina on 20 December 1860, rumors were rife that the Federal government would try to reinforce its forts in the lower South. All Southern governors in states with Federal forts contemplated seizure. On 2 January 1861 Governor Joseph E. Brown of Georgia telegraphed Moore that he had seized Fort Pulaski at Savannah and urged that Alabama seize its Federal forts. For several weeks Moore had been doing just that. Working through Thomas J. Butler, major general in command of the Alabama Militia, the governor asked Danville Leadbetter, a retired U.S. Army engineer, to survey the forts and make a report to him. The report declared that all of the forts were in disrepair and were only manned by skeletal forces.[19]

On 3 January Governor Moore issued orders for the state militia to seize the arsenal at Mount Vernon and Forts Morgan and Gaines in Mobile Bay. By 5 January these forts were all in Alabama's hands. Moore ordered that an overwhelming force be used in all cases as "it is all important that both the forts and arsenal shall be taken without bloodshed." The cooperationists condemned the seizure of the forts before the secession of the state, pointing out that not even South Carolina had been so lawless. Moore later told the convention that he had assumed "great responsibility. . . . For my justification, I rely upon the propriety and necessity of the course I have taken, and upon the wisdom and patriotism of the convention and people of Alabama."[20]

Even as he gave the orders for seizure, Moore was drafting a letter to President Buchanan. He explained the seizures as a precautionary measure taken upon evidence that the Federal government was moving to reinforce the forts.

---

[18]*The War of the Rebellion: A Compilation of the Official Records of the Union and Confederate Armies*, 128 vols. (Washington, 1880-1901), hereinafter cited as *OR*. Unless otherwise indicated, citations are to series 1. See series 4, vol. 1, 1-89; Roy R. Nichols, *The Disruption of American Democracy* (New York, 1948) 377 n. 553.

[19]Joseph E. Brown to Moore, 2 January 1861; Thomas J. Butler to Moore, 24, 25 December 1860; Danville Leadbetter to Moore, 28 December 1860.

[20]Moore to Col. J. B. Todd, First Regiment of Volunteers, General Order No. 1, 3 January 1861; Explanation of General Order No. 1 to Todd, 3 January 1861; Smith, *Debates*, 42, 49, 55.

By the move, the governor said, he hoped "to avoid and not to provoke hostilities." Moore further informed the president that an inventory of all Federal property had been ordered and that Federal property rights would be respected if peaceful relations continued. In late January Moore dispatched Thomas J. Judge to Washington to negotiate with Buchanan for a division of the public property and debt. Although Senator C. C. Clay used his good offices to urge Buchanan to see Judge, the president refused.[21]

After Lincoln's election, uncertainty regarding the future brought a financial crisis in its wake. On 4 December, Governor Moore issued a circular letter to all banks in the state pressuring them to suspend specie payments and to guarantee at least $1 million in their vaults to the state, to be allocated according to the capital stock of each bank. This was an emergency measure to be legalized later by the legislature, which Moore argued could not be called at the time because it would cause a run on the banks and defeat the purpose. Most of the banks suspended and all promised to guarantee their share to the state. In February 1861, the legislature authorized the earlier suspension on the condition that the banks purchase a fixed quota of state bonds at par value against which they could issue their notes. All banks suspended specie payments. Thus, the government secured nearly all the the specie in the state to finance the war in return for state bonds that were later to become worthless. Originally the state intended to begin paying interest on the bonds when specie payments were resumed, but this resumption did not occur during the course of the war. However, in 1861 the legislature changed its position and began paying the banks six percent interest on the bonds. Thus, the government financed itself at the beginning of the war by finagling the banks.[22]

In the meantime Governor Moore was seeking arms in a crisis atmosphere in which he had to compete with other Southern states and even foreign nations. Under the Military Bill passed by the last session of the legislature, volunteer companies were springing up in most of the counties in the state, and Moore was hard pressed to furnish them with arms. The folder marked "Military Affairs" in the Moore file in the Alabama De-

---

[21]Moore to President James Buchanan, 4 January 1861, in *OR,* vol. 1, 327; Smith, *Debates,* 41, 452-55; Ruth K. Nuermberger, *The Clays of Alabama* (Lexington, 1958) 181.

[22]Smith, *Debates,* 36-40; *OR,* ser. 4, vol. 1, 31-33; Walter L. Fleming, *Civil War and Reconstruction in Alabama* (New York, 1905) 162-63.

partment of Archives and History contains as many requests for arms as
for the commissioning of officers. The governor had several arms agents
in the field, but the most diligent was J. R. Powell, mail contractor, stage-
coach owner-promoter, and later a builder of Birmingham. Powell trav-
eled east to Washington, New York, and Boston in November and
December of 1860, purchasing $46,452 worth of arms, mostly small arms,
but including cannon, gun carriages, and caissons. His letters and tele-
grams to the governor present a vivid picture of frenzied buying by Southern states, with Georgia being first on the scene and the heaviest buyer.
The bulk of his purchases were from the Ames Manufacturing Company
in Massachusetts and the Tredegar Iron Works in Virginia. In several of
his letters he reported that Secretary of War John B. Floyd had been very
helpful to him in his quest for arms. On 25 November he wrote the governor from New York: ''I have been here several days and never have done
as much gun talk or heard as much in all my life.'' On 14 December Moore
called him home by telegraph, saying: ''Your purchase of muskets has created great dissatisfaction'' here. Actually his trip had received more publicity in the press, both North and South, than the governor or his agent
wanted. He wrote the governor at one point that ''if arrested north as an
incendiary you must take care of my wife and baby.'' From Boston he told
the governor, ''The ground you take is considered here very high ground.''
In the meantime Moore dispatched Quartermaster General R. T. Thom of
the Alabama Militia to New Orleans where he succeeded in buying 2,500
muskets and several hundred Colt pistols, along with some machinery for
producing arms and ammunition. The governor was also encouraged when
the owners of the Mobile Foundry reported to him that they were already
''rifling cannon and making shells for the use of the forts at the mouth of
Mobile Bay.'' This was to be only the beginning of the governor's quest
as he was besieged by volunteers, the Confederate government, and later
some of the border states for arms. When the war and the blockade began,
however, Moore's success in acquiring arms did not last.[23]

Governor Moore's relations with the secession convention were ami-
cable, perhaps because the immediate secessionists controlled the convention. The governor had telegraphed Commissioner J. A. Elmore to tell the

---

[23]J. R. Powell to Moore, 18, 20, 21, 25, 28, 29 November; 3, 4, 6, 7, 11, 14 December
1860; telegram, Moore to J. R. Powell 14 December 1860; T. R. Thom to Moore, 15, 16
November 1860; Skates and Company of the Mobile Foundry to Moore, 29 October 1861.

South Carolina convention to "listen to no proposition to compromise or delay" and had ordered the firing of a salute of one hundred guns when the news of the secession of that state reached Montgomery. He had promptly reported to and asked the blessings of the convention on his appointment of commissioners to the slaveholding states, his seizure of the forts and letter to Buchanan, his authorization to have the banks suspend specie payments, and his purchase of arms. When Governor Madison Perry of Florida called on Moore to send 500 armed troops and later 500 stands of arms to Pensacola, he was supported by a majority of the convention, which divided along immediate secessionist-cooperationist lines. Since the request for troops came before the passage of the Alabama Ordinance of Secession, the cooperationists argued that to comply would be an act of treason and war; the governor and the immediate secessionists countered that action was necessary because Pensacola was as important to the safety of Alabama as to Florida. When a stalemate developed at Pensacola and the cooperationists tried to recall the troops, the governor was supported by the same majority. The cooperationists struck back at Moore by introducing an ordinance based on the South Carolina plan that would create a council of state to advise him on military matters. This plan was defeated by a vote of fifty-two to forty.[24]

The governor called the legislature into special session on 14 January 1861 to implement actions taken by himself and the secession convention. The vote legalizing the suspension of specie payments and forcing each bank to buy a quota of state bonds passed the House by a margin of only forty-five to thirty-nine. In his message Governor Moore exhorted the legislature to place Alabama "as early . . . as possible upon the most efficient war footing." But this legislature made no attempt to reorganize the weak militia system. Volunteer companies were being organized in such numbers at this time that the legislature saw no serious need for a strong militia, which had been allowed to wither away after the removal of the Indians. However, these volunteer companies would soon be merged into the Confederate army, exposing the home front completely, and the lack of a strong home militia became one of the great issues of the war period—an issue never satisfactorily solved by Moore or his two successors. The legislature authorized the chief executive to issue treasury notes, an action that Moore,

---

[24]Smith, *Debates,* 52, 124, 161-63, 211-13.

unlike his successors, could largely ignore because the pressures of financing the war were not so immediate. The governor asked the House of Representatives to relinquish its chamber to the Confederate Convention, which opened on 4 February in a newly carpeted and generally refurbished hall.[25]

Moore had a ringside seat at the birth of a nation in Montgomery between 4 February and 21 May 1861, when the seat of the Confederate government was moved to Richmond. He could play host not only to the Alabama secession convention and the Alabama legislature but to the Confederate Convention and the Provisional Congress, all at the same time. Mary Chesnut, who mentions him on eight different occasions in her *Diary,* paints him as a graceful host, but something of a bore. As her *Diary* recorded her movements from one state affair to another, she depicted him as eager for companionship; and she must have known, although she does not say so, that Mrs. Moore was not with him because of mental illness.[26] The census of 1860 shows that Moore lived in the governor's house with his daughters Martha, who was twenty-two in 1860, and Anne, sixteen, and his only son, Andrew Barry, Jr., who was ten. The Confederate Congress seems to have been impressed with his hospitality. A member of that body wrote: "Governor Moore has treated us munificently, he has crowded our rooms with the best and most abundant stationery, and is treating the Congress with every manifestation of respect."[27] According to one account, Moore played a key role in the selection of Jefferson Davis to head the Confederacy. His two appointed commissioners to Virginia were authorized to pledge Alabama's presidential support for the conservative Davis over the "fire-eater" William L. Yancey (whom Virginians feared) in return for a secession convention in Virginia. Thus "the cooperation of Virginia and the border States" was assured, wrote Frank M. Gilmer, one of the commissioners.[28]

---

[25]*Journal of the Called Session of the House of Representatives,* 14 January 1861, 9, 57-59, 120, 123; *Acts of the Called Session,* January 1861, 9, 16.

[26]Mary Boykin Chesnut, *Mary Chesnut's Civil War,* ed. C. Vann Woodward (New Haven CT, 1981) 8, 9, 11, 20, 55, 56, 534.

[27]"Correspondence of T. R. R. Cobb, 1860-62," *Publications of the Southern Historical Association* 11 (May 1907): 160.

[28]F. M. Gilmer Memoir, May 1880, in Dunbar Rowland, ed., *Jefferson Davis, Constitutionalist: His Letters, Papers and Speeches,* 10 vols. (Jackson MS, 1923) 8:461-63.

Events moved rapidly during Governor Moore's last nine months in office, and the days were packed with administrative decisions. The legislature allowed him to hire an additional secretary to answer all of his mail. He requested that the legislature create a three-member military council (to serve at the pleasure of the governor) to advise him. He appointed and dismissed the council in short order, its members actually voting for their own dissolution. After dismissing the council, Moore made George Goldthwaite adjutant general of the state, a post in which he served with distinction under both Moore and his successor, John Gill Shorter. The governor appointed the able Duff Green, of Andrew Jackson's "kitchen cabinet" fame, quartermaster general of the state, a position he held throughout the war. Green played a vital role in Alabama's war effort, with both Shorter and his successor, Thomas H. Watts, adding to his duties. After authorization by the legislature, Moore dispatched J. W. Echols to the Northwest on a successful mission to buy commissary stores, realizing that a hungry army cannot fight. When Alabama troops became Confederate regulars, most of their state-purchased supplies and arms went with them.[29]

In the summer of 1861, the United States fleet blocked the inner channel between Mobile and New Orleans, and Moore, with the governors of Mississippi and Louisiana, was temporarily successful in opening it. When the owners of the *Florida,* a merchant vessel in Mobile Bay, did not agree to convert her to a gunboat under lease, the governor seized the vessel, leaving payment to a board of appraisers. In ordering the seizure, Moore said, "I shall not hesitate in taking the responsibility, confident that the state will sustain me."[30]

Many articles essential to life and health became very scarce early in the war, and speculators and extortioners appeared. In October 1861 Moore issued a proclamation: "I deem it my duty to protest, in this public manner, against such conduct, and pronounce it unpatriotic and wicked." The following month the Alabama legislature passed "An Act to Suppress Monopolies," imposing a fine and prison term for convicted speculators.

---

[29]*Acts of Called Session,* January 1861, 46-48; Governor's Message, *Senate Journal,* January 1861, 11, 17, 77. For Green's appointment, see Special Order No. 4, Moore's Order Book.

[30]Moore to Col. Percy Walker, 15 July 1861.

When the price of salt rose from one dollar to ten dollars a bushel, the governor without legislative warranty boldly designated a portion of the military fund for the purchase and distribution of salt to the poor families of soldiers. When speculators tried to run 1,400 sacks of salt to Columbus, Georgia, in an attempt to beat the legislative prohibition against out-of-state shipment, Moore seized the salt. He began leasing state-owned salt springs to private companies and individuals to encourage the production of salt. This practice introduced the first of many state home-front problems, which later reached crisis proportions. He attempted to solve the problem of indigent families of soldiers by having the legislature enact a provision allowing the courts of county commissioners to levy a local tax for the benefit of the indigent and to appoint agents to buy and distribute food.[31]

Ordinances passed by the secession convention allowed Moore to transfer the Federal forts and arsenal to Confederate ownership along with most of the arms captured at Mount Vernon, approximately 20,000 stands. The defense of the coast continued to be a major issue in the state. As large numbers of troops moved out of the state to the Virginia and Kentucky fronts, a clamor arose in southern Alabama that Mobile was being neglected and its fate was being left to the powerful United States fleet. The governor resisted all pressure "to make application for the recall of Alabama regiments in Virginia and Kentucky." However, after accepting two organized regiments from Mobile and the surrounding area, Moore declared that no more companies would be received from Mobile. He explained that fairness demanded that troops now come from other parts of the state as "Mobile is in the exposed position . . . and should have the means of protection constantly in reach." Privately the governor admitted that he was dissatisfied with the large number of troops leaving the state, and he threatened to treat as deserters all troops who resigned from state units to join the Confederate army.[32]

One historian, Frank Owsley, has charged Moore with creating a private army—thus denying much-needed troops to the Confederacy. Ows-

---

[31]Governor's Proclamation against Extortioners, 2 October 1861, in Frank Moore, ed., *The Rebellion Record,* 12 vols. (New York, 1861-1868) 3:159; Prattville *Autauga Citizen,* 14 November 1861; Bessie Martin, *Desertion of Alabama Troops* (New York, 1966) 170-71.

[32]Moore to Messrs. H. G. Humphries and Colin J. McRae, 16 July 1861; Moore to Col. Percy Walker, 3 July 1861; Moore to W. T. Ayers, 30 July 1861; J. W. Withers to Moore, 5 November 1861.

ley wrote: ''Governor A. B. Moore suggested to the legislature that Alabama should have a 'regular army' for its protection in case of trouble with the United States growing out of secession. A few days after this state convention adopted this suggestion . . . and authorized the organization of a state army. As a result, Moore was able in the fall of that year to report that the local troops—not to be confused with the militia—consisted of six regiments'' and other troops.[33] The ordinance of the convention, which Owsley refers to as proof that Governor Moore actually raised an army to the detriment of the Confederacy, was passed on 19 January 1861, when Alabama was a separate republic and the Confederate government not yet born. Therefore, the claim seems overdrawn, if not actually absurd. Troops of war were raised under the ordinance and sent to Pensacola, Mobile, and other points on the Gulf Coast at a time the Confederacy did not have troops there and had no way of getting them there. As the Confederacy gained organization and strength, Alabama troops (with their arms) were phased into the Confederate army. In fact, Alabama was filling a vacuum that the Confederacy was incapable of filling at the time.

When the governor of Florida called for aid, Moore rushed the Second Regiment of Alabama Volunteers, under the command of Tennent Lomax, to Pensacola. On 13 January, two days after Alabama left the Union, Lomax was instructed to assume command, if offered, and to take Fort Pickens even ''at a sacrifice.'' But Governor Madison Perry of Florida placed William H. Chase, an old army officer who had built Fort Pickens, in command, and Alabamians jokingly said that Chase did not want to take the fort because he did not want to show that it was pregnable. Moore did not give up. When he dispatched the First Regiment of Alabama Artillery to Pensacola on 7 February, he instructed Commander John H. Forney to get command, but the opportunity never came. The governor declared Fort Pickens ''of first importance to the safety of the seceding states of the Gulf of Mexico. No other place on the Gulf is safe,'' he said, ''while the federal troops hold possession of the commanding fortifications at Pensacola.'' Moore found it exasperating not to have command at Pensacola, so close to the Alabama line and a place where most of the troops were Alabamians. Alabama troops, few of whom were regulars, found it even more ex-

---

[33]Frank L. Owsley, *State Rights in the Confederacy* (Chicago, 1925) 25.

asperating to be called away from the farm, shop, or office just to "do nothing."[34]

Scholars have said that after secession all factions came together (even in northern Alabama) to support the Confederacy until the war became too long and too hard. Moore's correspondence contradicts that position. On 16 July 1861, a citizen of Blount County wrote that "a very considerable number of the inhabitants of the counties in Winston, Marion and Morgan are disaffected toward the Confederate government and are actually raising and equipping themselves to sustain the old government of the United States." Other letters add Lamar, Walker, Shelby, Randolph, and Tuscaloosa counties to the list of those with disaffected people. On 12 July a justice of the peace in Lamar County wrote Moore of a class of people "hurrahing for Lincoln and saying that they will fight for him and even forming companies to protect themselves against our government." Moore, worried and wondering whether to use force in putting down the opposition, dispatched ex-congressman and future governor George S. Houston to the area. Houston thought force was unnecessary and, in fact, told the governor that the worst thing he could do was to send in troops recruited from northern Alabama counties because of existing regional factionalisms. During the crisis, Moore wrote to one of his informers in Walker County, "I say to you emphatically that as long as I am governor of the state the laws against treason and sedition shall be faithfully executed if it takes the whole military power." Huntsville's Jeremiah Clemens, ex-United States senator and Mexican War veteran, whom Moore had appointed major general of the Alabama Militia in an effort to placate the cooperationists, went over to the enemy after the capture of Huntsville in April 1862.[35]

---

[34]Moore to William M. Brooks, 12 January 1861, *OR,* vol. 52, pt. 2, 5; J. J. Seibels, Moore's aide-de-camp, to Tennent Lomax, 13 January, Ibid., 11; J. J. Seibels to John H. Forney, 7 February 1861, Ibid., 17; Tennent Lomax to Moore, 27 July 1861.

[35]W. Hunsgrove to Moore, 16 July 1861; J. H. Vail to Moore, 9 July 1861; Houston to Moore, 1, 27 August 1861; Moore to Josephus W. Hampton, 12 July 1861. For letters from all the counties named, see folder marked "Sedition" in Moore Collection. *Savannah News,* 24 May 1862. For a contrary interpretation, see Moore, *History of Alabama,* 428-29. See also Hugh S. Bailey, "Disloyalty in Early Confederate Alabama," *Journal of Southern History* 23 (November 1957): 522-28. Thornton, *Politics and Power,* 437. Thornton points to disagreement on the subject but prefers the older view that Alabamians were united for war in 1861.

Volunteers were plentiful in the early months of the war, but arms were so scarce that Moore had the sheriffs of each county search among the people for old militia arms. Troop units vied for arms and marching orders from the governor, and some wrote him bitter letters when disappointed. Although Moore received calls from army generals and border state politicians begging for arms, most of the pressure came from the Confederate government. Some scholars have criticized Moore and other southern governors for not turning over all arms to the Confederacy. He turned over arms from the Federal arsenal, but kept and allocated the arms purchased by the state. In Moore's defense, he did arm many units who went into the Confederate army but, in part because of public clamor, he also kept arms at home that were needed badly elsewhere. Ironically, Moore's states' rights policy, like that of other Southern governors, prevented a centralized effort to arm the Confederate army. Another states' rights policy that helped to cripple the Confederacy was at issue in his refusal to allow state agents to collect Confederate taxes.[36]

In December of 1861 Moore proudly told his last legislature, "Your state has given to the defense of the confederacy full 27,000 of her men." He said that twenty-three regiments were already in the field and five others near completion. "Of these troops Alabama has armed more than 14,000 and equipped nearly half that number," Moore declared. In closing he told the legislators, "As my official connection with the state will soon be dissolved it is a source of much gratification to be able to say that there is no state in the Confederacy which has done more in proportion to its means . . . to aid the Confederate government . . . than Alabama."[37]

On 2 December 1861 Moore's second term came to an end, and he was prohibited by the Alabama constitution from succeeding himself. He left the governorship, but did not give up on the war effort. He worked tirelessly as special aide to his successor, John Gill Shorter. Shorter sent him to northern Alabama to recruit and rush troops and supplies to Albert Sid-

---

[36]A. S. Johnston to Moore, 15 September 1861, *OR,* vol. 4, 408; Moore to Braxton Bragg, 8 November 1861; S. B. Buckner to Moore, 15 September 1861; Judah P. Benjamin to Braxton Bragg, 4 November 1861, *OR,* vol. 6, 440; Governor's Message to Legislature, *OR,* ser. 4, vol. 1, 698. For criticism of Moore on the arms issue, see Owsley, *State Rights,* 10-11.

[37]*Journal of the Second Called Session of the Senate* (Montgomery, 1862), 9, 20, 29-30.

ney Johnston, to western Alabama to persuade planters to furnish slave labor for the completion of the Alabama and Mississippi Railroad, to the Black Belt to buy corn for indigent families of soldiers, and to various other trouble spots. Forsaking party lines, Moore even lent his good offices to the Watts administration. In 1864 he bought corn in the Black Belt at less than market level for Governor Watts to distribute to the needy. During this turbulent period, Moore's health began to fail and, at one point, he was dangerously ill. During the latter part of the war, he lived quietly at his home in Marion. The ex-governor must have endured some painful soul-searching as he watched the collapse of the Confederacy, including the fall of nearby Mobile. He, like so many others, had believed that lack of cotton in the British textile industry would force England to intervene in favor of the Confederacy. In February, 1862, he warned Jefferson Davis not to allow any cotton to leave the port of Mobile.[38]

The end came with Lee's surrender at Appomattox in early April, followed by Johnston's on 26 April in North Carolina, and Richard Taylor's on 4 May in Alabamá. On 16 May 1865, Secretary of War Edwin M. Stanton ordered General E. R. S. Canby to "arrest and imprison Moore, the person lately claiming to act as Governor of the State of Alabama, and keep him confined in a secure military prison." The correspondence concerning the arrest and imprisonment of Moore, "the secession governor," shows a bitterness not displayed toward his two successors. He was arrested at or near his home in Marion and taken by way of Montgomery and Mobile to New Orleans, where he was sent by steamer to Fort Pulaski in Savannah.[39] The Montgomery *Mail* of 3 June 1865 reported that "Ex-Governor Moore of this state was carried through our city several days since under guard. . . . He is in feeble health." Moore was detained at Fort Pulaski for a few months and released in August 1865, in part because of his failing health.[40]

---

[38]John Gill Shorter to Moore making him a colonel and aide-de-camp, 12 December 1861; Shorter to Col. Moore, 28 December 1861, 9, 24 March 1862, 10 February 1863; Moore to Shorter, 24 October 1862, in *OR*, ser. 4, vol. 2, 148-49; Governor Moore to Jefferson Davis, 3 February 1862, in *OR*, ser. 4, vol. 1, 905.

[39]Edwin M. Stanton to General E. R. S. Canby, 16 May 1865 in *OR*, vol. 49, pt. 2, 810. For further correspondence in regard to Moore, see *OR*, ser. 2, vol. 8, 648.

[40]Owen, *Alabama*, 4: 1222.

He came back to Marion where he practiced law until his death on 5 April 1873. He was buried in the Fairview Cemetery in Perry County.[41]

The Civil War had overtaken Moore. However, Moore could rest peacefully knowing that his successor, John Gill Shorter, was a man who also worked for, and firmly shared, Moore's belief that secession was the best answer to the South's problems.

---

[41]Obituary and articles in Montgomery *Advertiser and Mail*, 6 April 1873.

CHAPTER II

JOHN GILL SHORTER:
Longtime Secessionist

John Gill Shorter, the second of the three wartime governors of Alabama, was born in Monticello, Georgia, on 3 April 1818. His father, Dr. Reuben Shorter, a physician and planter, had come from Virginia to Georgia as a young man and had become a leader of the rising Jacksonian party. In 1833, with a restlessness typical of the period, he moved to Irvinton (now Eufaula) in what was to become Barbour County, Alabama. John Gill graduated from the University of Georgia in 1837 and followed his father to Eufaula where he was admitted to the bar the next year. In 1843 he married Mary Jane Battle, the daughter of a wealthy Barbour County planter.

John Gill and two of his brothers attained prominence in Alabama politics. Eli Sims Shorter served two terms in the United States Congress (1855-1859), and a younger brother, Henry Russell, was a member of the Railroad Commission (1888-1897). In the 1840s, the Shorters became large landholders in Barbour's rich Black Belt. The law firm of John Gill and Eli Shorter prospered and became the most prominent in southeastern Alabama. In 1844 Governor Benjamin Fitzpatrick appointed John Shorter solicitor for the Eufaula District and the next year he was elected to the state Senate as a Democrat although Barbour County generally elected

Whigs. In the Senate Shorter quickly won a reputation for independence of thought and, as a contemporary legislator and historian wrote, his minority reports from committees established his "readiness to follow his conviction, though it separate him from his fellow members." In other words, he did not play politics under any circumstances. When his term ended, he refused to run again for the Senate but in 1851 was persuaded to become a candidate for a seat in the lower house. He was elected, but soon gave up his seat when Governor Henry Collier appointed him circuit judge of the Eufaula District. In 1852, he was elected to the same judgeship, and six years later he was reelected.[1]

On the issue of Southern rights, Shorter became a disciple of William L. Yancey and an admirer of John C. Calhoun. In 1850 he was a delegate from Alabama to the Nashville Convention and an ardent secessionist. At a Southern rights convention held in Montgomery in March 1852, he warned the yeomanry that unless they supported the planters on the racial issue they stood to lose more than the planters. If four million slaves were turned loose in the South, he said, the rich "would be able to leave a land thus cursed, [while] the poor white man would be left in a most lamentable condition . . . reduced to the most abject and degrading servitude."[2]

Throughout the 1850s Shorter was a member of the so-called Eufaula Regency (consisting of about a dozen lawyer-planters in Barbour County), which first came together in a bipartisan effort to elect Zachary Taylor president in 1848. Although Jefferson Buford might be called the leader of the regency, John Shorter and his brother Eli were key members. The Shorters belonged to the Democratic rather than the Whig wing of the regency. Next to the radical Montgomery group, the Eufaulians were the most influential in taking the state out of the Union in 1861. One historian has called the Eufaula group "the most consistent secessionists in the state during the fifties."[3]

Perhaps because of a busy schedule as circuit judge, Shorter did not offer to be a delegate to the secession convention. However, Governor

---

[1]Hallie Farmer, "John Gill Shorter" in Allen Johnson and Dumas Malone, eds., *Dictionary of American Biography*, 20 vols. (New York, 1928-1937) 17:129-30; Garrett, *Reminiscences*, 722-23; Brewer, *Alabama*, 126; Ralph N. Brannen, "John Gill Shorter: War Governor of Alabama, 1861-1863" (Master's thesis, Auburn University, 1956) 1-90.

[2]Quoted in Thornton, *Politics and Power*, 207.

[3]Dorman, *Party Politics*, 36.

Moore sent him as commissioner to Georgia to urge the cooperation and secession of that state. He had grown to manhood in Georgia, was a graduate of its university and, although he lived in Alabama, his plantation was across the Chattahoochee in Quitman County, Georgia. As he told Governor Brown, he was a "delegate from Alabama, the beloved State of my adoption, to Georgia, the beloved and honored State of my nativity." Arriving in Milledgeville in early January 1861, he appealed to Georgians through a letter to Governor Brown to "unite with Alabama and sister States in throwing off the insolent despotism of the North, and in the establishment of a Southern confederacy . . . which shall endure through all coming time." On 16 January he sent a message to the Georgia Secession Convention "inviting the people of Georgia and of the other slave-holding States to meet the people of Alabama, by their delegates, in convention on the 4th day of February, 1861, at the city of Montgomery." He was the first Alabamian to invite the Confederate states to have their convention in Montgomery.[4]

Shorter was elected to the Provisional Congress of the Confederate States while still in Milledgeville—one of two Yanceyites elected out of an Alabama delegation of nine, as the secession convention, in an act of self-denial, generally passed over its own members in an effort to secure the support of the cooperationists. Shorter served in the Confederate Congress in Montgomery and Richmond until he left to become governor of Alabama in December 1861. As a member of Congress he was active in framing the Confederate constitution and was chairman of the Engrossments Committee. He performed his share of routine business and took the initiative in policy making in having Congress acknowledge that the states owned all public lands within their borders. He was the sponsor of the most important compromise in the debate on the permanent Confederate constitution. There were bitter arguments between the radicals and the moderates over whether to admit states without slavery to the new union. The radicals, wishing to protect slavery above all else, sought to limit the Confederacy to slave states; the moderates, looking to the strength of the new Confederacy, wanted to expand into the West and even Mexico. Some actually envisioned the admission of the states of the Old Northwest, such as

---

[4]Shorter to Governor Joseph E. Brown, 3 January 1861, in *OR,* ser. 4, vol. 1, 16-17; Shorter to George W. Cranford, president of the Georgia Secession Convention, ibid., 54-55.

Illinois. The Shorter Compromise provided for the admission of all future states by a two-thirds vote of the House of Representatives and the Senate, with each state having one vote in the Senate. After the convention became the Provisional Congress, Shorter was a consistent supporter of President Davis. As a congressman, he actively carried the Confederate cause to the people. At Montgomery in June 1861 he appealed to Alabama planters to invest as much of their cotton crops as possible in government bonds so that Confederate troops could be armed and equipped.[5]

Alabamians were divided over the approaching gubernatorial election that was set for the first Monday in August. The major issue of the year had just been settled in the secession convention that removed the state from the Union. It was obvious that this issue might be reopened in any heated campaign where candidates were nominated by the usual convention method, were run on a platform, and were allowed to canvas by election-eering and exhorting the voters. As a party, the Democrats were embar-rassed by the situation. They could muster the party machinery to hold county, district, and state conventions, have the convention adopt a plat-form, and nominate a candidate for governor. Their candidate would prob-ably be elected, but their opponents could not do this and the very act of this election process placed them in a partisan position. Faced with inde-cision, they allowed the issue to drift. Democratic party attempts to hold county conventions in Lowndes and Calhoun counties in the summer of 1861 were abandoned because local leaders were indecisive and the state organization was aimless. Many newspapers wanted "politics as usual" suspended during the war. They suggested that the usual conventions, platforms, and electioneering be abandoned in order to achieve enough unity and strength to win the war. When the war was over, they could af-ford to resume their differences.[6]

Five candidates were nominated for governor by newspapers across the state in 1861. They are listed in the order of their support and hence im-portance: John Gill Shorter of Eufaula, Thomas H. Watts of Montgomery, John E. Moore of Florence, Robert Jemison, Jr. of Tuscaloosa and Thomas

---

[5]Thornton, *Politics and Power,* 435; Brannen, "Shorter," 10; Montgomery *Weekly Advertiser,* 15 June 1861; Emory M. Thomas, *The Confederate Nation* (New York, 1979) 65.

[6]Jacksonville *Republican,* 15, 27 June 1861; Brannen, "Shorter," 12-21.

J. Judge of Montgomery, who was Watts's law partner. Judge had only local support in Lowndes and Montgomery counties, and was one of the first to withdraw. Jemison, who was from Tuscaloosa but also had some strength in Mobile, soon withdrew, saying that his background as a co-operationist would only cause discord in the election. Many northern Alabama newspapers were persistent in their support for John E. Moore, claiming that he could win because Shorter and Watts would cancel each other out in central and south Alabama. Moore withdrew in early July. But Moore's withdrawal was not a gracious one. He declared that since north Alabama had not had a governor in more than fourteen years and since he was the runner-up to A. B. Moore in the last convention in 1857, he thought "as a matter of courtesy" the nomination in 1861 should go to north Alabama. In supporting Moore, the north Alabama press had much to say about the neglect of that section by the politicians of central and south Alabama. They declared that there was an unwritten rule by which the governorship would be alternated between north and south Alabama and that this rule had been violated by south Alabama since the elevation of A. B. Moore to the governorship in 1857. John E. Moore's withdrawal left only Shorter and Watts in the race. However, shortly after Moore's withdrawal, Watts also issued a similar letter saying that he did not wish "to scramble for the office" and further divide public opinion in the state.[7]

The Montgomery *Post,* in nominating Thomas H. Watts for governor in 1861, presented him as an ideal candidate around whom all the people of Alabama could rally. In fact, such a candidate did not exist because of the nature of the situation. Watts was a very able man but had been aligned throughout his political life with the Whig party, which had never won a gubernatorial election in the state.[8]

From the beginning, Shorter's candidacy had the most statewide support. In May 1861 Shorter was petitioned to run for governor by about 200 of his friends and neighbors from Barbour and the surrounding counties. The Eufaula Regency, with Eufaula *Spirit of the South* as spokesman, had initiated the petition. This newspaper had been dedicated to the formation

---

[7]Florence *Gazette,* 2, 10, 13, 24, 30 July 1861; Huntsville *Democrat,* 24 July 1861; Mobile *Tribune,* 8 July 1861; Montgomery *Weekly Confederation,* 10 July 1861; Brannen, "Shorter," 12-21.

[8]Montgomery *Daily Post,* 3, 26 June; 19, 24 July 1861.

of a Southern union since 1850 when its editor dropped the appellation *Democrat*, saying, "Because Whig and Democrat are distinctions which no longer live in spirit, they should no longer live in name." Although Shorter had major newspaper support in central Alabama (also Watts country) and southern Alabama, he was also supported by newspapers in northern Alabama, where the Jacksonville *Republican* editorialized in supporting him that "no man ought to suffer his name to be run, who has not been known as a thorough-going secessionist" for years. This qualification fit Shorter but eliminated all other candidates. Another northern Alabama newspaper which offered Shorter fervent support was the Huntsville *Democrat*, edited by John Withers Clay, the brother of C. C. Clay.[9]

The press was generally divided along previous party lines and carried on a confused political campaign while the candidates remained silent for fear that they would be charged with undermining the war effort by playing politics. Each side called on the other's candidate to withdraw in the name of patriotism. Shorter remained in the Provisional Congress in Richmond and did not answer the opposition press, and Watts kept busy organizing the Seventeenth Alabama Regiment without a word about politics. Watts wrote his withdrawal letter on 10 June, but when his press support persisted, he issued a statement on 3 August, five days before the election, saying that if elected he would serve. Actually, by attempting to withdraw from the race and then reentering it, Watts campaigned more than Shorter. The most important aspect of the entire campaign was that it was a farce; the electorate knew nothing about the political intentions of either candidate. The press discussed personal issues regarding the alleged strong and weak points of each candidate's character. The charge that Shorter had a "hankering for office," since he was running for the office of governor when he already had the high office of congressman, was typical.

On 8 August Shorter was elected by a vote of 37,849 to 28,121, a majority of nearly 10,000. The returns typified most of the elections held in Alabama since the rise of the party system in Andrew Jackson's day. The Democrats, led by Shorter, won large majorities in northern Alabama while

---

[9]Rhoda Coleman Ellison, *History and Bibliography of Alabama Newspapers in the Nineteenth Century* (University AL, 1954) 52; Jacksonville *Republican*, 15 June 1861; Huntsville *Democrat*, 24 July 1861. The Jacksonville *Republican*, 27 June 1861, contains a full account of the Barbour County petition to Shorter to become a candidate and his written reply.

the Whigs, led by Watts, were victorious in the Black Belt and the rich river counties of southwestern Alabama. The only variation from this was Shorter's substantial favorite-son vote in southeastern Alabama. The question of secession was not an issue in the election. The electorate apparently was not thinking about the war—or, if they were, it was mostly about the Battle of First Manassas, which was a Confederate victory. However, the geopolitics of Shorter's vote did not furnish him with a good basis of support for the war effort during the next two years. In fact, many who supported him would be behind Union lines within six months and other supporters would be under attack from close range, with Shorter helpless to do anything about it. Ironically, Shorter, the longtime secessionist, had been elected governor of Alabama by the antisecessionists. In other words, membership in the Democratic party was more important than the issue of secession in winning this election. The voting tally in large towns reveals that Watts won 1,843 to 434 in Montgomery, 1,776 to 464 in Mobile, and 1,115 to 150 in Dallas, while Shorter won 1,195 to 37 in Madison, 1,274 to 496 in Tuscaloosa, and 1,524 to 373 in Barbour (Shorter's Black Belt county home).[10]

Shorter, at forty-three, was inaugurated as the seventeenth governor of Alabama on 2 December 1861. Those who crowded the hall of the House saw a man "of ordinary height, with a delicate figure and intellectual cast of features" assume the oath of office. His inaugural address called for building state fortifications and the war industry. He said that industry was needed to win the war and that the Confederacy was fighting to gain not only independence, but also "a deliverance, full and unrestricted, from all commercial dependence upon, as well as from all social and political complications with, a people who appreciate neither the value of liberty nor the sanctity of compacts." It was a hard-line address in which he said, "Our coasts may be ravaged, our cities and towns reduced to ashes . . . but the sacred right of self-government, inherited from our fathers and stamped with their life's blood, Alabamians never will surrender." He spoke of "unaccustomed burdens" that the war would bring but, as he later said, he scarcely knew the trials that he and the people would have to endure. A very conscientious and religious man, he closed by invoking "the blessing

---

[10]Election results in *Journal of the House of Representatives* (Called and Second Regular Annual Sessions, 1862) 117-18; Brannen, "Shorter," 12-18; Malcolm C. McMillan, ed., *The Alabama Confederate Reader* (University AL, 1963) 233.

of God, whose favor we implore'' to bring liberty and freedom to the people of the Confederacy.[11]

Shorter's first priority in office was to strengthen the forces of Albert Sidney Johnston. Johnston's situation in Tennessee and Kentucky was desperate and he asked Governor Moore, before his term ended, to send as many troops as possible from northern Alabama. As we have seen, Shorter appointed ex-Governor Moore to be a military aide with the rank of colonel. Moore was sent to raise and arm troops in that section. Two regiments and a battalion were formed, and Shorter indicated to Johnston that many more could be sent if arms were available. Five hundred slave laborers, the first of thousands recruited under Shorter, were sent to work on fortifications at Tennessee's Fort Henry. Nonetheless, the Kentucky and Tennessee fronts crumbled rapidly and in February 1862, after the fall of Fort Henry, the first invasion of Alabama soil occurred during a gunboat raid up the Tennessee River to Florence. Incredibly, the worst was yet to come. Shorter was only in office four months before news reached Montgomery that Alabama, north of the Tennessee River, was being occupied by the Federal army of General O. M. Mitchel. Thus, that section of the state where secessionist sentiment was least popular had become, as some of its leaders predicted, the first to suffer the rigors of civil war. Except for a brief respite in the fall and winter of 1862-1863, this area, which was predominantly Democratic and which had supported Shorter for governor in 1861, was a battlefield. Likewise, the mountainous pro-Shorter counties to the south of the Tennessee, although not occupied, were the scene of constant forays across the river. In September 1862, calling for Confederate help, Shorter wrote the secretary of war that the enemy was increasing its devastation south of the river and in a ''few weeks . . . will have devastated the most fertile and wealthy part of the Valley.'' Significantly, the horrors of war in the area turned the political situation completely around by 1863.[12]

---

[11]Shorter's Inaugural Address, in *OR*, ser. 4, vol.1, 771-74; Brewer, *Alabama*, 126-27.

[12]A. S. Johnston to Shorter, 13 December 1861, in *OR*, vol. 7, 762-63; Shorter, Circular Address to the People of Alabama, 13 July 1863, in Montgomery *Weekly Advertiser*, 15 July 1863 (Shorter's review of his administration to date in answer to his critics, hereinafter cited as ''Address''); Brannen, ''Shorter,'' 22-23; Shorter to Randolph, 3 September 1862. All Shorter letters cited without *OR* derivation are in the Shorter Collection, ADAH.

In April 1862, when northern Alabama was invaded, Shorter called for the formation of four partisan cavalry companies to harass the enemy and contain any raids that the enemy launched south of the Tennessee River. The volunteers would provide their own horses and arms, but be fed and clothed by the state. The governor knew that arms were not currently available, so he warned each volunteer to bring, in addition to twenty rounds of ammunition, "his bullet moulds and powder flask." Shorter said that the state had no arms but that "if the men cannot provide themselves the state will furnish each man with a large bowie knife"—thus revealing the truly desperate arms situation. The Federal movement into northern Alabama came so quickly and with such surprise that the governor and the people were initially stunned by the news. There was a two-week lapse between the enemy occupation and the governor's proclamation, a time lag for which he was later criticized. However, the governor was completely dependent upon the Confederate cavalry to defend northern Alabama because of the Army of Tennessee defeat at Shiloh and the concentration of troops in Virginia. At Shorter's request, John Tyler Morgan, who had raised a regiment of cavalry for the eastern Tennessee front, was ordered to northern Alabama by the Confederate secretary of war to help Philip D. Roddy, who was already organizing the defense of the valley. Morgan's troops were only partially armed and completely lacked a commissary or quartermaster department. The governor sent him ammunition and $25,000 for supplies by ex-Governor Moore and called on the Confederates at Chattanooga to supply arms.[13]

However, before Morgan was ready to act, the Federals on 31 August temporarily withdrew from the Tennessee Valley, fearing their lines of communication would be cut by Braxton Bragg's invasion of Tennessee. They left behind a bitter people who could not forget that their valley had been invaded and much of it destroyed. When reports of the ruthless invaders, including the "rape of Athens," reached Montgomery, the governor was powerless to help. In January 1863, before the return of the enemy, Shorter made his only trip to the valley to assure the people of his interest and to persuade them to form volunteer units for local defense. From Decatur he went to Tullahoma, Tennessee, where he visited General

---

[13]Brannen, "Shorter," 23-24; Shorter, "Address"; Shorter to John Tyler Morgan, 2 September 1862; Shorter to Major General Barclay, 12 February 1862; Shorter to C. C. Clay, 22 March 1862; Governor's Proclamation Book, 12 February 1862, in ADAH.

Bragg, whom he greatly admired, and received the general's pledge to do anything he could for the protection of northern Alabama. But when he returned to Montgomery because of the pressure of business, instead of going down the valley to survey the devastation, the people of the valley were greatly offended. Later, a citizen of the area asked Shorter's successor, Thomas H. Watts, to come there in person and not to send an aide, a course "which your immediate predecessor sometimes adopted to discharge his official functions."[14]

Governor Shorter's correspondence indicates that during his first months in office he spent hours each day on plans for the defense of Mobile and Pensacola. Like A. B. Moore, he considered the defense of Pensacola as important to Alabama as to Florida and "opposed the abandonment of Pensacola so long as there was the slightest hope of holding it." In early March 1862, after hearing that the Confederate government planned an early evacuation of Pensacola, he visited the city and realized that it would be physically impossible to remove the guns, ammunition and other public stores—worth millions to the Confederacy—unless the order to evacuate was postponed. By joint telegram with the officer in command to the secretary of war, he was able to postpone the order. He sought and received the cooperation of the governors of Mississippi and Georgia in delaying evacuation of the city and he proposed to the secretary of war that Pensacola be made an instruction camp where 5,000 or more troops would be kept in training before being sent to other fronts. He wrote Secretary of War Randolph that "Pensacola, next to Norfolk, is the most important point on our seaboard" because of its fine harbor and healthy location. He thought "that 50,000 men would not be able to repair the loss of a port which 5,000 could now hold safely." He argued that since much of the border country was lost, middle Alabama was now the "breadbasket" of the Confederacy and asked: "What are we to do for food if middle Alabama is seriously disturbed?" Shorter sent seventeen companies from Confederate regiments being formed in Alabama to Pensacola.[15]

Finally, Pensacola had to be evacuated. When the removal of cannon, heavy machinery, and other government property was ordered for security

---

[14]Edward C. Betts to Thomas H. Watts, 5 February 1864, in ADAH.

[15]Shorter to Judah P. Benjamin, 18 March 1862; Shorter to G. W. Randolph, 5 April 1862.

reasons, Shorter called on planters to furnish slave labor to repair the Alabama and Florida Railroad so that these goods could be brought to Alabama. After the goods were removed, the governor ordered the track between Pensacola and Pollard torn up to prevent its use by the enemy. Those who argued for evacuation said that the troops and big guns at Pensacola would be more useful in defending points in the west. Although an opponent of evacuation, Shorter sought and secured his share of Pensacola's cannon to fortify Mobile and the river defenses of the Alabama and the Tombigbee. On 10 May 1862 Pensacola was evacuated, and Shorter protested to a close friend, ''The administration evidently considers success at Corinth and in Virginia the great end to be accomplished, and to secure this result, have made up their minds to give up less important positions.'' Nevertheless, Shorter had delayed the evacuation of the city, a delay that not only made possible the removal of heavy war materials worth millions to the Confederacy, but allowed many private citizens fleeing to southern Alabama towns to get out with their private possessions.[16]

The failure of the Confederacy to save Pensacola plagued Shorter. He feared, with good reason, that the Confederacy might also remove its forces from Mobile and concentrate them elsewhere. In a later address to the people he declared that the military disaster at Shiloh and the retreat to Corinth brought the abandonment of Pensacola and the occupation of northern Alabama, in addition to the withdrawal of Confederate land forces from Mobile. Thus, only the forts at the mouth of the bay were garrisoned. Bragg's army, which had been defending Mobile and Pensacola, was sent to Tennessee; Shorter advised that Alabama ''must supply a state force sufficient to defend the city against a land attack'' from the Federal fleet, which at the time was landing troops on Ship Island, equidistant between Mobile and New Orleans. There was great excitement and confusion in Mobile with much talk that the city had been left to the mercies of the Federal fleet. It was a trying time for the governor and the people of southern Alabama. Shorter immediately urged the secretary of war to send the war regiments forming in the state to Mobile. The state militia joined them also, called from Mobile and nearby counties, but its strength was severely weakened

---

[16]Shorter to F. H. Shepherd, 13 May 1862; Shorter, ''Address.''

because so many of its members had volunteered for the Confederate army.[17]

Tension eased somewhat after the capture of New Orleans, and Shorter allowed some militia units to return home if they turned over their arms to the state. The governor used these guns to arm the Confederate regiments forming in Mobile. Although most of the arms were quite inferior, and the state paid the owners, charges were made that the governor had unnecessarily called up the militia and that it was "a mere pretext or scheme to obtain their arms." Shorter replied that he allowed the militia to return home because every able-bodied man needed to be on the farm in April and he thought it "highly inexpedient to send militia to Mobile with arms and to hold war troops at the same point without arms." The charge was probably inevitable, given the scarcity of even old muskets and the tensions of the crisis. Shorter was also blamed because, in an effort to organize the defense of the city, some of the militiamen were mustered into the Confederate army. The strong defenses later built around Mobile did not exist at this time, and the city was saved only because the enemy chose to attack New Orleans.[18]

Although Mobile was safe for the present, the controversy over the defenses of the city continued. The Mobile Committee of Public Safety, chaired by Peter Hamilton, pressured Shorter throughout his administration to make Mobile secure. The governor, in turn, pressured the Confederate government. Shorter wrote the secretary of war, "Our Gulf coast is abandoned to the enemy. . . . We are destitute here now, having sent out of the state all the public arms the state had, and contributed them, with our brave troops, to the common cause. . . . I earnestly insist upon every possible contribution for the defense of Mobile and the Alabama River."[19] After Shorter wrote pleading letters, Jefferson Davis tried to placate the governor by agreeing to "the immense importance of Mobile" but arguing that inferior numbers of Confederate troops dictated their use elsewhere unless Mobile was threatened with imminent attack. The president re-

---

[17]Shorter, "Address"; Shorter to Brigadier General Thomas S. Butler, 20 December 1861; Shorter to Judah P. Benjamin, 13 January 1862; Braxton Bragg to Shorter, 31 December 1861.

[18]Shorter, "Address."

[19]Shorter to Benjamin, 4 March 1862, *OR*, vol. 52, pt. 2, 281-82.

ferred to Shorter's previous support and asked for his continuing "friendly cooperation, which has already been cheerfully rendered."[20]

Linked with the defense of Mobile was the continued scarcity of arms. Like Governor Moore, Shorter thought the state government had been generous in allowing the Confederacy so many arms at its disposal and carried on an extensive correspondence with the secretary of war concerning the matter. The governor wrote the secretary of war on 5 March 1862, "our difficulty is not in procuring men but arms and ammunition." The secretary replied on 17 March that he was "almost in despair at the call for arms for all parts of the Confederacy, which it is totally out of my power to give." On 23 March Shorter telegraphed the secretary, "I have not a single regiment which has arms and equipment, hardly clothing and but one which has tents. I have no arms." In addition to the 20,000 stands of arms captured at Mount Vernon, Shorter wrote that the Confederacy had been the recipient of 18,000 stands used to arm Alabama troops sent to the Virginia and Tennessee fronts. These troops and arms were gone, he said, and Mobile "left entirely to the mercies of the Yankee fleet in the Gulf."[21]

Shorter asked the Alabama legislature to give him power to impress arms, but the legislature refused on the grounds that the possession of arms was a sacred right of the people. Nevertheless, the governor insisted that all arms issued to the militia over the years were the property of the state. In addition, he appealed to the people to give or sell their arms to the state. Shorter, like Moore, sent agents throughout Alabama to gather militia muskets and to purchase "country arms" of all kinds, including double-barreled shotguns and even flintlock rifles, which could be bored or altered from flint to percussion if the barrel was at least an inch in diameter.[22]

In December 1861 the legislature appropriated $250,000 for the governor to purchase arms, but all arms from abroad had to run the blockade. The governor therefore turned to home manufacture of small arms. Shops and small foundries in Mobile, Montgomery, Selma, Fayetteville, Talla-

---

[20]Jefferson Davis to Shorter, 29 October 1862, in Rowland, *Davis Letters,* 5:361.

[21]Shorter to Benjamin, 5, 23 March 1862; Benjamin to Shorter, 17 March 1862; Shorter to Randolph, 5 May 1862, in *OR,* vol. 2, pt. 2, 281-82.

[22]Shorter to T. H. Claiborne, 15 December 1862; Shorter to William Alley, 25 January 1862; Shorter to Brig. Gen. Thomas J. Butler, 25 February 1862; Proclamation Book, 1 March 1862.

dega, Opelika, and other points throughout the state were contracted to manufacture or repair arms. Special manufacturing-only contracts were awarded to Dickson Nelson and Company of Tuscumbia, the Arms Manufacturing Company in Talladega, and the Fayetteville Gun Manufacturing Company of Fayetteville. In February 1862, before Tuscumbia was overrun by the enemy in April, Dickson Nelson and Company secured permission from Shorter to move its plant to Rome, Georgia. However, shortly after the plant was reconstructed in Rome, much of it was destroyed by fire. The capital to build and operate these companies was supplied by the state. The largest contract was made with the newly formed Alabama Arms Manufacturing Company in Montgomery, to whom the state gave $250,000, which was to be paid back in manufactured arms. However, despite all of the governor's options, the arming of Alabama troops remained a major unresolved problem. Some eighteen months after the contracts were let, Shorter reported to the legislature that no arms had been delivered to the state by any of the contractors. He assigned the failure by the companies to deliver arms on time to the lack of skilled mechanics. Although he had generally recommended for detail all conscripted skilled mechanics, his requests were denied by the secretary of war.[23]

The Confederacy resorted to conscription in April 1862 in order to keep an army in the field. Although the Federal army continued to press on all fronts, overrunning Kentucky, Tennessee, and the northern parts of Mississippi and Alabama, volunteers were slow to reenlist in 1862. Many Confederate leaders called for conscription. Initially, Shorter opposed conscription on the grounds that the war could be won only by "men of deep devotion to liberty." "If we are to depend upon [conscription] to maintain the liberty of the South, I should almost despair of our ultimate triumph," he said. After conscription became law, the governor counseled the secretary of war that "the enrollment should be postponed as long as possible until the grain and provision crops" could be gathered. This was especially important in northern Alabama, the granary of the state, where opposition to the law was most pronounced. However, when conscription became effective, Shorter used all the powers of his office to support it. There was no struggle between the state and the Confederacy over con-

---

[23]*Acts of Alabama* (Second Called and First Regular Session, 1861), 75; *Journal of the House* (Called and Third Regular Session, 1863) 49-50; Brannen, "Shorter," 49; Shorter to F. H. Shepherd, 13 May 1862.

scription such as occurred under Shorter's successor. Shorter was anxious to use state enrolling officers, an alternative to Confederate officers, to enroll conscripts because conscription "can be more effectually made by our own officers," he said, "than by imported officers from the army who will be apt from their manner and bearing . . . to render the execution of the conscript law obnoxious to the people." However, the conscription law provided that the state enrolling officers would have the same rank and pay of the state militia enrolling officers, which did not exist in Alabama. Despite the governor's enthusiasm for state officers, the secretary of war, after some correspondence, ruled, on constitutional grounds, that his only alternative was to use Confederate enrolling officers. Although disappointed, Shorter graciously acquiesced.[24]

Shorter correctly predicted the opposition to conscription in the mountain counties of northern Alabama and the Wiregrass of southeast Alabama. Armed resistance to conscription first occurred in Randolph County in September 1862, and afterwards broke out sporadically there and elsewhere. The Confederate War Department immediately sought Shorter's advice on handling the situation without bloodshed, suggesting that he might send in a force commanded by state officers. The governor replied that he would sustain the law with all moral force but that, from the beginning, conscription had been "discharged and directed solely by Confederate officers, and under these circumstances I question the policy of calling in State officers." He suggested that the cavalry be used to enforce the law, but said that "the law should be enforced at every hazard." Confederate cavalry moved into Randolph, and the trouble subsided. However, three months later Shorter telegraphed the secretary of war, "Randolph County defies enforcement of conscript act; an armed force made jailer surrender keys and liberated deserters. . . . I say again, speedy action is necessary or deserters from every quarter will increase. Unreliable conscripts from this State should be sent to Virginia at once." He suggested that such troops be sent as far away from home as possible, but the deserters in Randolph County would not cease their activities. More than a year after Shorter dispatched the latter message, the Columbus *Times* reported that there were upwards of four hundred deserters in the county or-

---

[24]Shorter to Randolph, 30 May, 24 June 1862; Shorter to Lieut. Col. John F. M. Morgan, 14 February 1862; Shorter, "Address to the Legislature," in *Journal of the Senate* (Called Session and Second Regular Annual Session, 1862) 18.

ganized into a battalion for the purpose of "carrying on a systematic warfare upon conscript officers."[25]

Violence was by no means the only way to express opposition to conscription. Letters to the governor described the methods being used in Covington County. "Deputy clerks" and "deputy sheriffs" became numerous; others formed "little schools although they could not write their names"; and still others "procured little mail routes." One letter said that the war was a "rich man's war and a poor man's fight" because only the rich and influential could evade conscription. The writer asked the governor to see that conscription was administered fairly, and Shorter wrote at the bottom of the letter for his secretary to answer, "Confederate law—duty of the enrolling officers to look after its execution. Governor has nothing to do with it." Many people were inclined to blame all unpopular Confederate measures on the executives of their state, and this time Shorter's reaction was uncharacteristically blunt.[26]

During his governorship, Shorter nurtured the University of Alabama and in 1862 made it a military school. The governor called on the La-Grange Military Institute to turn over its arms to the state, which he rushed to Fort Henry to bolster Albert Sidney Johnston's forces. On the other hand, he sent more arms to the University of Alabama, which he frequently called "our military nursery." The university had instituted the military system of discipline and training in 1859 as a partial result of the martial spirit provoked by John Brown's raid. After the fall of Fort Donelson, there was an exodus of cadets from the university that stopped only when Shorter intervened and refused to accept them in the president's call for twelve new regiments. Instead, he ordered the cadets to twelve camps of instruction where they became military instructors for raw recruits. It was Shorter's determination that cadets should remain in Alabama as instructors of recruits that kept the university open during the war. Shorter sent university president L. C. Garland to Richmond to present the case for the university before Jefferson Davis. Garland carried a letter from the gov-

[25]Shorter to Sec. of War Randolph, 19 September 1862, in *OR*, ser. 4, vol. 2, 87; Shorter to Sec. of War Seddon, ibid., 258; and Inspector General Samuel Cooper to Shorter, 24 December 1862, ibid.; Montgomery *Weekly Mail*, 21 October 1863, quoting the Columbus (GA) *Times*.

[26]W. G. Porter to Shorter, 24 August 1862; James M. K. Little to Shorter, 1 September 1862.

ernor asserting that, among other things, the university cadets had trained
some 12,000 of the 18,000 troops raised in the state since he took office.
Although the Exemption Act of April 1862 did not specifically exempt the
cadets, Shorter boldly declared that they were a military unit under his
control, commissioned under the Great Seal of the state, and were not subject to the Conscription Act. The secretary of war never agreed to the governor's position but, perhaps because it made sense, the cadets continued
as drillmasters during the war and the university remained open.[27]

Perhaps no problem on the home front worried Governor Shorter more
than the growing number of indigent families of soldiers. Many were on a
starvation diet and were without salt to preserve food. Bessie Martin, in
her *Desertion of Alabama Troops,* found that suffering families at home
were the major cause for the desertion of Alabama troops. Even conscientious soldiers placed their duty to family above their duty to the state. In
the summer of 1862, Shorter began receiving letters from probate judges
and justices of the peace in several counties telling him that hundreds of
soldiers' families faced starvation unless the state furnished relief. In October 1862 the governor called a special session of the legislature for the
purpose of making provision for the indigent families of soldiers. Shorter
appealed to the legislature to provide for the families of volunteers and
conscripts alike, and said that the 1861 levy for the indigent, providing
twenty-five percent on top of the state property tax, was insufficient and
that the state must support the families of those dying for the cause. The
legislature appropriated $2 million to be disbursed by the comptroller to
the probate judges of all counties, who were to distribute the relief under
the supervision of the county commissioner courts. One of the most important aspects of the law provided that the probate judge in each county
make a survey of the needs of soldiers' families and report the findings to
the state as the basis for future relief. Realizing that care of the indigent
was a local matter in the first place, the legislature passed—and the governor signed—a bill empowering the county commissioners to levy an ad-

---

[27]"Report to the Board of Trustees," in *Journal of the House* (Called and Second Regular Annual Session, 1862) 148-49; Shorter to Lieut. Col. Nicholas Davis, 4 December
1862; Shorter to Corps of Cadets, 21 February 1862; Shorter to Randolph, 28 April 1862;
Shorter to Jefferson Davis, 1 May 1862.

ditional local tax for the indigent, without which there could have been no effective program.[28]

The survey showed that indigent families had increased from one in ten during 1862 to three in ten during 1863, and when Shorter went before the legislature in November 1863 he called upon the lawmakers to make an appropriation on the basis of the increasing need. The legislature appropriated $3 million to be divided into four quarterly installments among the counties on the basis of the number of their indigents. The governor was authorized to use any unappropriated funds in the treasury or, if necessary, to issue more treasury notes. Earlier in 1862, when the sale of bonds failed to finance the $2 million appropriation for the indigent, the first treasury notes had been issued. For the $3 million, Shorter had to issue more treasury notes which, because they fed inflation, meant that when relief finally reached the indigent, the notes would be worth much less than when the money was appropriated. As money decreased in value, Shorter placed more emphasis on the purchase of supplies by the state for distribution. This was usually impractical because of transportation problems. Shorter, like Moore, placed purchasing agents in the field to make purchases at reasonable prices in order to thwart speculators. For example, in 1863 the governor bought, through his special agent ex-Governor Moore, corn in the Black Belt at $1.25 a bushel when the going market price was $3.00. Grain was plentiful in the Black Belt throughout the war, but the state's inadequate railroad system was now overburdened with war goods, and transportation of relief supplies was often impossible. Shorter threatened to impress teams to haul grain from the Black Belt to counties in northern Alabama, although there were no records indicating that he actually did this. The "corn women" from north Alabama, walking with sacks on their backs, were a familiar sight in the Black Belt by 1863. They were given corn by the planters, and much of the relief was on the private or county level, without which the state's program would have been totally inadequate.[29]

---

[28]S. K. Rayburn to Shorter, 11 July 1862; Charles Gibson to Shorter, 30 September 1862; Governor's Message in the *Journal of the Senate* (Called and Second Regular Annual Session, 1862) 210-15; Martin, *Desertion,* 121-65; *Acts of Alabama* (Called and Second Regular Annual Session, 1862) 17-18. Phyllis L. LeGrand, "Destitution and Relief of the Indigent Soldiers' Families of Alabama During the Civil War" (Master's thesis, Auburn University, 1964) is the best study of the problem.

[29]Martin, *Desertion,* 170-75.

Mobile, the largest city in the state, had many indigent families, but local organizations took the burden off the state in caring for them. The Military Aid Society of Mobile employed soldiers' wives to make uniforms that had been contracted for by the government. The Soldiers Relief Association was probably the most helpful relief association in Mobile. It organized the Free Market and dispensed as much as $120,000 in goods to indigent families in 1862 and $200,000 in 1863. Similar associations were organized in Montgomery and Selma, but they were never as effective as those in Mobile.[30]

During the winter of 1862-1863, a dearth of provisions existed in Mobile after Lieutenant General John C. Pemberton of the Army of Mississippi issued an order forbidding the shipment of grain and other provisions out of Mississippi so that his own army might be well supplied. After construction of the Mobile and Ohio Railroad, Mobile depended on provisions from northern and eastern Mississippi for much of its food. The Mobile Committee of Public Safety contacted Shorter, asking him to get the order rescinded. Shorter wrote General Joseph E. Johnston, commander of the Department of the West, asking him to rescind the order, but Johnston refused to interfere. Shorter then wrote Pemberton and he too refused to rescind or modify the order. The commanders told Shorter to bring provisions by boat from the rich river counties of Alabama, but he replied that Alabama planters were not prepared, on a minute's notice, to get provisions over the almost impassable winter roads to the boat landing on the rivers. Eventually, trade could be rerouted and an adequate supply obtained, but that would take time.[31]

During late summer of 1863, the warehouses of Mobile merchants were depleted. The scarcity of supplies was caused by the Pemberton embargo on goods from Mississippi and by the increasingly effective Federal blockade of Mobile. For Mobile, an urban area inhabited by 25,000 people, an effective system of transportation and distribution was imperative. The

---

[30]Ibid., 163-66.

[31]Shorter to Peter Hamilton, Chairman, Mobile Committee of Public Safety, 25 February 1863; Shorter to Lieut. Gen. John C. Pemberton, 28 February 1863. T. A. Hamilton, secretary of the Mobile Supply Association, asked the governor to suspend the State Extortion Act in order that famine-stricken Mobile could buy at any price, but Shorter replied that he did not think suspension of the act would help. See Shorter to T. A. Hamilton, 28 February 1863.

horrible lack of food and clothing compelled the women of Mobile to riot in September 1863. One vivid account describes the scene as follows: "The women of Mobile, Ala., rendered desperate by their sufferings met in large numbers on Spring Hill road with banners on which was [*sic*] printed such devices as 'Bread or Blood' on one side and 'Bread and Peace' on the other, and armed with knives and hatchets, marched down Dauphine Street, breaking open the stores in their progress, and taking for themselves such articles of food and clothing as they were in need of." Although news of this riot was suppressed by the Confederate press, reports of it reached the Northern press where it was cited as evidence that the South was crumbling from within.[32]

Because of his Northern birth, Pemberton was already suspect in the minds of many Confederates, and his arbitrary allocation of supplies from Mississippi brought further hatred of him in Alabama.

The Mobile Committee of Public Safety sent a petition to Shorter calling for Pemberton's removal after the fall of Vicksburg in July 1863. Shorter sent the petition to President Davis with a letter stating that the petition did not stem from "sentiments of pique or ill will" but instead repeated "the universal testimony of the Vicksburg army." He added that "the criticism may be unjust to Gen. Pemberton but it is so." He deprecated the fact that counties already filled "with deserters and a restless uneasy population" would soon be filled also "with the dissatisfied spirit of the army of Vicksburg." Thousands of Alabama soldiers were paroled after Vicksburg's fall and made their way across Mississippi to their homes in Alabama.[33]

Closely allied to the problem of feeding the indigent was the task of producing an adequate supply of food for all. This crucial task involved keeping prices reasonable and discouraging extortion and speculation. On 1 March 1862 Shorter proclaimed to the people, "Plant not one seed of cotton beyond your home wants, but put down your land in grain and every other kind . . . of farm product and raise every kind of livestock." In the same proclamation he denounced "vile extortion, which is a sin against humanity." He announced his intention of placing a tax on any cotton grown beyond home needs and seed for the next year. In December 1862, some eight months later, the legislature, upon the governor's recommen-

---

[32]For further details, see McMillan, *The Alabama Confederate Reader*, 335-36.

[33]Shorter to Jefferson Davis, 8 August 1863.

dation, imposed a tax of ten cents per pound on all cotton grown above 2,500 pounds of seed cotton per worker. The governor later said that the law should have been even more stringent.[34]

Shorter, like Moore, believed that if British cotton mills were denied Southern cotton, England would eventually be forced into the war on the side of the Confederacy. When blockade-runners started fitting out river steamers for running cotton through the blockade to Cuba, he made a strong protest to Secretary of War Seddon and Major General Simon B. Buckner, commander at Mobile. Shorter pointed out that, in addition to his opposition to their carrying cotton from Mobile, all the vessels would eventually be destroyed and there would be no way to move the army, guns, food, and other supplies on Alabama's inland waterways.[35]

To keep grain and other food from being used by distillers, Shorter, as a war measure and on his own authority, stopped the distillation of ardent spirits in Alabama as of 1 April 1862, except that which he would license for medicinal and war purposes. Since the right to make liquor was a proverbial one in the frontier South, this measure met with some opposition. Hard liquor of a better-than-local grade had been shipped south from the Northwest grain belt before the war, but this trade had been stopped by the blockade. In issuing his proclamation, Shorter said that wartime distillation had been prohibited in Tennessee and Georgia, thus driving distillers into Alabama, where they were "converting food necessary to sustain our armies and people into poison to demoralize and destroy them." Although the ban was presented as a war measure, the wording of the proclamation gave it prohibitionist overtones. Anxious for legislative backing, Shorter took the issue to the next session of the legislature, which in December 1862 gave the governor the right "to have distilled only such amount of grain as he thinks consistent with the common defense and the general welfare of the state." Under the law, the governor licensed distillers to make alcohol for medicinal and manufacturing purposes in those counties where a surplus of grain existed. Applications were numerous and the law be-

---

[34]Shorter, Proclamation, 1 March 1862 in Governor's Proclamation Book, 35; *Acts of Alabama* (Called and Second Regular Annual Session, 1862), 43-44; Brannen, "Shorter," 56; E. Merton Coulter, *The Confederate States of America, 1861-1865* (Baton Rouge, 1950) 240.

[35]Shorter to James A. Seddon, 28 March 1863, in *OR*, ser. 4, vol. 2, 461; Shorter to Maj. Gen. S. B. Buckner, 28 March 1863, Ibid., 462-63.

came very difficult to enforce. A license fee was placed on distillers to be used for the support of indigent families. This fee, according to the governor, would bring in about $150,000 annually.[36]

Shorter attacked the wartime salt-scarcity problem the same way he approached all issues. He determined what he felt was the right course and worked tirelessly, regardless of self or politics, to fulfill his goal. His zeal for the production of salt was so great that he was criticized by some of his contemporaries, who felt that his energies should have been spent securing arms. However, that criticism ignores two important facts: (1) the arming of troops was the major responsibility of the Confederacy, and (2) Shorter made extensive contracts for arms. The actual threat of a "salt famine" was very real to him and the people, if not his critics. He wrote so many letters and issued so many directives on this matter that his files contain more material on it than on any other subject. Indeed, as cooperative as Shorter was with the Confederate government, he challenged it immediately in May 1862 when some Liverpool salt that belonged to Alabama was impressed by a Confederate agent in Memphis. Although he did not get the same salt back, the Confederacy soon replaced it with Virginia salt. When the blockade began, several thousand sacks of Liverpool salt belonging to Alabama were caught in New Orleans. Shorter wrote Governor Thomas O. Moore of Louisiana about the salt and sent Duff Green, quartermaster general of Alabama, to New Orleans. Green managed to get the salt to Alabama.[37]

Salt was very cheap before the war because it was shipped in large amounts as ballast on ships from Europe that carried cotton on the return trip. The blockade forced every state in the Confederacy to find a new supply, and this took time. Because salt was so important as a preservative before the age of refrigeration and was in dwindling supply, it became the first article of trade to be cornered by the speculators. Prices rose from sixty-five cents a bushel in 1860 to $20 in 1862 when Shorter was writing about a "salt famine." Alabama was fortunate in that it had the second-largest known supply in the Confederacy on reservations in Clarke County in the

---

[36]*Acts of Alabama* (Called and Second Regular Annual Session, 1862), 43-44; Shorter's Proclamation in Troy *Southern Advertiser,* 28 March 1862; Brannen, "Shorter," 59-60; Paul W. Gates, *Agriculture and the Civil War* (New York, 1965) 97.

[37]Shorter to Governor Thomas Moore, 31 December 1861, 7 June 1862; Shorter to Duff Green, 11 July 1862; Brannen, "Shorter," 60-61.

southwestern part of the state. These lands, which had been given the state when Alabama entered the Union, bordered on the Tombigbee River. The largest supply was in Virginia, with Saltville at its center, and a large supply of rock salt was discovered in Louisiana during the war.[38]

In early 1862 Shorter leased to P. Figh and Company the lower part of the state reservation, which became known as the Lower Works. He advanced the company $10,000 that it was to pay back in salt. Figh agreed to supply the state with salt at $1.25 per bushel of fifty pounds, ten cents of which was a subsidy to the company from the state. Shorter realized that the Figh salt would not adequately supply even the indigent families of soldiers, who were to receive all of it, so he visited the salt reservations with the idea of having the state go into the salt business. He authorized J. Darby, a chemist living in Auburn, to make a survey of the reservations. Darby found Alabama salines to be weaker than those in Virginia, but their use was both necessary and profitable. In May 1862, the governor appointed A. G. McGehee to be salt commissioner for the State Works and sent him to study the Virginia wells at Saltville. McGehee returned to Alabama and built the state plant, called the Upper Works, and began its operation in October 1862 with a total capacity of nearly 600 bushels a day.[39]

The legislature endorsed the governor's move to place the state in the salt manufacturing business in the fall of that year. Shorter even recommended to the legislature that the state take possession of any private company that was unwilling to confine itself to "reasonable profits," but that step, although it occurred in Virginia, was never necessary in Alabama. However, the governor used the threat of seizure to speed up production. He told a Clarke County salt company in April 1862, "I, as executive of the state will feel it my duty to seize your works as a military necessity, that the same may be made completely subservient to the public welfare." The struggle ended when the state bought most of the company's lease. The threat of seizure by the state shows the extent to which the war had forced the governor to change his laissez-faire philosophy of the prewar

---

[38]Ella Lonn, *Salt in the Confederacy* (New York, 1933) 18-21, 129-30; Governor's Message to the Legislature, in *Journal of the Senate* (Called and Second Regular Annual Session, 1862), 10-14.

[39]Shorter to Messrs. P. Figh and Company, 24 May 1862; Darby's Report to the Governor, 13 May 1862; Shorter to Adj. Gen. Duff Green, 7 June 1862; Shorter's Salt Circular, 30 June 1862, in Shorter Papers, ADAH.

era. The war created a veritable revolution in the economic affairs of Alabama and all the Southern states. Alabama entered into manufacturing directly and indirectly (through the subsidization of manufacturers by the state), actions unthinkable to antebellum Alabamians.[40]

In June 1862, Shorter, by circular letter, opened the remaining salt reservations to all Alabamians, an order that he later amended to include all citizens of the Confederacy. They were invited and even urged to come and make salt for their families; a license from the governor was, however, required to produce salt for sale. In late 1862 the Confederacy, faced with the problem of furnishing salt to its armies, contacted Shorter about making salt in Alabama. At the governor's request, the legislature authorized him to lease twenty acres to the Confederacy. However, as it turned out, the Confederacy needed 100 acres to make salt by solar evaporation. The legislature had already adjourned, but Shorter assured the secretary of war that he would provide the space required for evaporation and that he felt confident the next session of the legislature would endorse the agreement. However, the Confederacy never proceeded with the project.[41]

The governor was also active in searching for salt outside the state. He made a contract to obtain salt from the newly discovered rock-salt beds in Louisiana, but the project was thwarted by Federal gunboats on the Mississippi and, finally, by the fall of Vicksburg, which cut off the Confederacy west of the river. Since northern Alabama was not connected by water or rail with southern Alabama, Shorter moved to have salt made in Virginia for the indigent living in northern Alabama. This salt could be shipped on rail lines through Knoxville or Atlanta. He entered into a salt-making contract with the Virginia Works, a contract that was passed on to a Knoxville company. The state advanced the company $10,000 and the state was to be paid back in salt. To insure the company from loss, the state obligated itself to buy 100,000 bushels at $1.75 per bushel, a price that rose to $3.00 a few months later because of the rapid deterioration of currency. However, the very problem the governor was trying to avoid arose to plague

---

[40]Shorter to Messrs. Dennis, English, and Thomas, 22 April, 14 May 1862; Governor's Message, *Journal of the Senate* (Called and Third Regular Annual Session, 1863), 85; Brannen, "Shorter," 60-61; Emory M. Thomas, *The Confederacy as a Revolutionary Experience* (Englewood Cliffs NJ, 1971) 71-72.

[41]Shorter's Salt Circular, 30 June 1862; *Acts of Alabama* (Called and Second Regular Annual Session, 1862), 56; Lonn, *Salt*, 76.

him. War pressure prevented the railroads from carrying the load, and salt destined for northern Alabama often failed to arrive, despite the valiant efforts of an Alabama agent in Virginia and a transportation agent for the state who rode the rails. Weeks went by while Alabama salt was neglected in favor of Confederate and Virginia freight. Shorter protested directly to the secretary of war, but salt continued to move only sporadically through Knoxville until Federal forces cut the rail lines in late 1863. The salt was then routed through Atlanta until that line was cut in 1864. The governor tried every known expedient to get the salt to Alabama. On at least one occasion, he hired a special train to bring salt to the state.[42]

Some clashes between civil and military authorities occurred in Alabama while Shorter was the chief executive. Shorter made every effort to support Confederate officials in the state, but took offense at any deliberate disregard of private rights or contempt for state authority. One such complaint involved a Confederate military officer who illegally arrested the probate judge of Pike County after he entered a decision against the military in the case of a county officer who was claimed as a conscript. Shorter immediately contacted the secretary of war, who ordered the judge released, but only after the state press had "crucified" the military.[43] Another incident pitting the military against the civil government occurred when General Dabney H. Maury, who replaced General Buckner as the military commander at Mobile, closed all grogshops and saloons in the area in the interest of the discipline and sobriety of the soldiers. The merchants of Mobile protested to the governor, who informed the commander that the order was an invasion of state authority and should be revoked. Shorter suggested placing a sentry at every grogshop instead. Maury immediately revoked the order.[44]

---

[42]Shorter's Salt Circular, 30 June 1862; Shorter to Duff Green, 2 January, 14 November 1863; Shorter to Messrs, Stewart, Buchanan, and Co., Saltville, Va.; Shorter to James A. Speed, 19 December 1862; Shorter to Capt. A. Snodgrass, 4 August 1863; Governor's Message, *Journal of the Senate* (Called and Third Regular Session, 1863), 86; Sec. of War Randolph to Shorter, in *OR*, ser. 4, vol. 2, 175; Lonn, *Salt*, 90, 114, 140.

[43]Montgomery *Weekly Advertiser*, 11 November 1863; Shorter to editor of Mobile *Tribune*, 29 October 1863, releasing all the correspondence about the case.

[44]The Protest of George Kendall and Other Merchants to Shorter, 20 October 1863; Shorter to Gen. Dabney H. Maury, 28 October 1863; Shorter to Peter Hamilton, 28 October 1863; Governor's Message, *Journal of the Senate* (Called and Third Regular Annual Session, 1863), 92.

One of the bitterest clashes between the military and civil authorities occurred in Tuscaloosa, where Federal prisoners were being held early in the war. Confederate authorities first incensed the governor by suggesting that the newly completed insane asylum was an ideal place to house the prisoners. Shorter wrote to Dr. Peter Bryce and his board of trustees that they should "positively refuse the asylum, consecrated to suffering humanity, to be polluted by the footprints of our insolent invaders." He telegraphed Secretary of War Judah P. Benjamin, "Better send no more prisoners to Tuscaloosa—accommodations exhausted—Lunatic Asylum will not be leased—To seize it would disorganize the institution and would arouse the just indignation of a loyal and Christian people." The prisoners were housed elsewhere, but the large number of prisoners and their guards disrupted the local economy and government, and Tuscaloosa was placed under martial law. Too many people needed to be fed, and supplies became depleted. Under pressure from the governor, the prisoners were finally removed and martial law was suspended, but the people of Tuscaloosa remained disconsolate.[45]

Another clash between civil and military authority was averted when a rumor about Confederate seizure of stores at the university commissary never materialized. When word reached Shorter that Confederate officers might impress some of the commissary stores, he wrote President Garland, "It cannot be tolerated and if one shall be found so rash as to attempt such an unauthorized procedure, such an outrage upon the state University, you will be expected to resist him promptly by every measure at your command." Fortunately, Confederate agents did not attach university stores.[46]

One of the issues that contributed to Shorter's defeat in 1863 was his vigorous impressment of slave labor for war work. Although the legislature did not pass an act giving the governor the power to impress slaves for such purpose until October 1862, Shorter used emergency power to act until that time. At the beginning of the war many planters offered free slave labor to the state and Confederate governments. In December 1861 ex-

---

[45]Shorter to Sec. of War Benjamin, 18, 21 December 1861; Shorter to Dr. Peter Bryce, 19 December 1861; Sec. Randolph to Shorter, 5 May 1862; Shorter to Gen. John Forney, 7 May 1862.

[46]Shorter to Dr. L. C. Garland, 28 June 1862.

Governor Moore, as Shorter's agent, easily obtained 500 slaves in northern Alabama to work on the fortifications at Fort Henry, which was out of state—a fact that might have drawn criticism. In October 1862, however, the otherwise loyal planters of west-central Alabama began withdrawing their slaves from work on the Alabama and Mississippi Railroad (Selma to Meridian), which the Confederacy was pushing as a war necessity. Complaints were already circulating about alleged abuses to which impressed slaves were being subjected, including charges of neglect in subsistence and sickness. Shorter, at first, contended that impressed slaves were treated better than soldiers. He said that "while receiving double the pay . . . they have been better fed . . . and sickness has not been as much as the average sickness amongst the same number of soldiers."

Shorter sent Moore, probably his most indispensable aide, to west Alabama to make peace with the planters, and he persuaded them to furnish labor to rush the railroad to completion. Slaves were impressed by the governor to grade the Alabama and Tennessee Railroad above Blue Mountain and a portion of the North and South Railroad but after 1862 the scarcity of iron rails prohibited any further projection of railroads. Although there are other cases involving the forced use of slaves for railroad work, this use was small when contrasted with the thousands impressed to build the fortifications at Mobile.[47]

Many slaves were also impressed to build the defenses blocking the Alabama and Tombigbee rivers at Choctaw Bluff and Oven Bluff. After Federal gunboats were easily able to take forts on the Mississippi River and its tributaries, defense preparations on the rivers that led into the heartland of Alabama became almost an obsession with the governor and his advisors. Obstructions were to be placed at strategic points on the rivers to impede enemy gunboats so that they could be destroyed by cannon from the bluff above. More points would have been fortified, but Shorter said the concentration at Oven Bluff and Choctaw Bluff was forced by the scarcity of cannon. The greatest fear, shared by the governor and the people of central and southern Alabama, was that Alabama would be invaded

---

[47]Sec. Randolph to Shorter, 2, 29 October 1862, in *OR*, ser. 4, vol. 2, 106; A. B. Moore to Shorter, ibid., 148-49; Shorter to L. Gibbons, 4 March 1863; Governor's Proclamation to the Planters of Alabama, 16 March 1863.

through Mobile. Their fears were quite valid because it was impossible for them to know that this would not occur.[48]

The slaves working in Mobile represented the largest number of impressed laborers, and they were requisitioned through the governor by the military commanders of that city; and the work was paid for by the Confederate government, but the pay was about as dependable as soldiers' pay. The state paid the owners of most of the slaves who worked on the river obstructions, but those requisitioned by Confederate engineers were paid by that government. In February 1863 5,000 slaves were requisitioned for Mobile and 2,100 for the river works. In October 1863 Shorter needed 4,000 more slaves for work on Mobile's defenses. The governor, with some difficulty, tried to enforce the state impressment law, which provided for an overseer for every thirty slaves, forbade impressment from any owner with fewer than ten slaves, and limited the work of any impressed slave to sixty days a year.[49]

On 14 August 1863 Shorter wrote General Maury, commander at Mobile, that "since I have been in office, there have been impressed under my orders upwards of 10,000 slaves, not to mention wagons, mules etc." In retrospect, he estimated that by conservative calculation "there have been fully five hundred deaths, in many instances caused by sheer neglect." Shorter repeatedly exhorted the military commanders to care for the slaves, but the commanders were first of all interested in finishing the job. Among those he requisitioned for the commanders at Mobile, he said, there were cases where no records were kept, where the slaves were underfed and not returned on time, where sick slaves were neglected, and where wagons and tools were destroyed so that they could not be returned. Shovels, wagon teams, and tools were so scarce that requisition from the planters was the government's main source of supply, yet the planters needed the wagons,

---

[48]In a letter to General Samuel F. Buckner, 3 March 1863, Shorter recounts all the slaves that he has impressed for the defenses of Mobile and the fortification of the bluffs. The letters about these fortifications are too numerous to cite. Shorter to Brig. Gen. S. B. Buckner, 3 March 1863, and Shorter to L. Gibbons, 4 March 1863, are representative letters.

[49]*Acts of Alabama* (Called and Second Regular Annual Session, 1862), 37-40; Governor's Message, *Journal of the Senate* (Called and Second Regular Session, 1862), 8-9. The Confederate Impressment Act of March 1863 left the provisions of the State Impressment Acts still in force.

teams, tools, and slaves in season if the Confederate people and armies were to be fed.[50]

The impressment of slaves became so unpopular that Shorter was faced with the resignation of many of his impressment agents and the refusal of others to take their places. After passage of the Confederate Impressment Act of 26 March 1863, the governor's correspondence indicates that he wondered whether he should continue to take the blame or let the Confederate government impress the slaves directly. However, he was so involved by that time that he apparently felt it was a matter of honor and patriotism to continue. After his defeat Shorter wrote that the impressment of slaves ''to the extent that I have felt it my duty to do was the strongest element which carried the state so largely against me.'' In other areas, Shorter appears to have been basically opposed to impressment. He wrote to Robert M. Patton, one of his aides in northern Alabama, that he would much prefer buying cloth from a Tennessee Valley mill rather than attempt impressment.[51]

State aid to the Confederacy was an outgrowth of the emphasis on states' rights. Shorter was among the first Confederate governors, if not the first, to offer state aid in the supply of Confederate troops. In *State Rights in the Confederacy* Frank L. Owsley condemned this practice as being very harmful to a concentrated war effort because it denied the Confederate government control of supplies for the good of the whole army. The system also brought higher prices in the marketplace, where each Confederate state and the Confederate government competed for goods. On 1 August 1862 Governor Shorter wrote Secretary of War Randolph offering to help supply clothing for Alabama troops in the coming winter. Most of the troops, he said, were not conditioned to the colder climates of Virginia and Tennessee. The Confederacy accepted the offer, and the Alabama legislature in November 1862 appropriated $250,000 for the manufacture or purchase of 50,000 pairs of shoes for Alabama troops. The appropriation bill gave the governor the right to impress all goods for their manufacture. Shorter had pointed out to the secretary that leather and wool from Texas

---

[50]Shorter to Gen. S. B. Buckner, 3 March 1863; Shorter to Gen. Dabney H. Maury, 14 August 1863.

[51]Shorter to Robert M. Patton, 13 September 1862; Shorter to Dabney H. Maury, 14 August 1863.

were now almost impossible to secure. The state was to supply the shoes but be reimbursed by the Confederate government. As it turned out, the Confederate government bought them at a higher price than cost; the state made $100,000 on the arrangement. Each state's supply of its troops became a common practice throughout the Confederacy, and from Owsley's account it appears to have been worse in many states than in Alabama.[52]

Although there can be little doubt that the practice got so completely out of hand that the war effort was impeded, state pride in supplying troops with clothing through the Ladies Aid Societies must be considered a positive factor. Shorter reported to the same legislature that appropriated $250,000 for shoes that the Aid Societies in the last year had supplied Alabama troops with 6,102 overcoats, 16,024 jackets, 17,387 pants, 19,230 shirts, 16,535 drawers, 7,002 hats, 6,257 blankets, 11,979 pairs of socks, and 10,798 pairs of shoes, besides many other articles.[53]

The heavy emphasis on state aid was apparent in many aspects of the Southern war effort. Governor Moore had established a hospital in Richmond for Alabama troops, and Shorter continued to give the hospital his wholehearted support. As large numbers of Alabamians lay wounded, sick, or dying in Corinth, Mississippi, under deplorable conditions after the Battle of Shiloh, Shorter was prompted to establish an Alabama hospital at West Point, Mississippi. During its brief existence, it became known as the Alabama Army of Mississippi Hospital. Shorter placed Dr. F. A. Bates of Marion, Alabama, in charge of the hospital and sent his aide, ex-Governor Moore, to the site to help Bates organize it. The state purchased lumber and other stores and had completed two buildings when it became apparent that the fighting in the west could not be contained nearby, and the hospital had to be abandoned. Shorter, and later his successor, encouraged the establishment of hospitals or, more often, rest homes for Alabama soldiers in many of the towns and villages of the state. State aid in some areas had only positive effects on the Confederate war effort. Under Shorter, the Alabama legislature was the first to pass a resolution that the state guarantee

---

[52]Owsley, *State Rights*, 113-27. See *OR*, ser. 4, vol. 2, 32, 196, 235, for correspondence between Shorter and the secretaries of war about troop supply.

[53]Governor's Message, *Journal of the Senate* (November 1862), 76.

the payment of all Confederate debts—an effort to bolster Confederate credit desired by Secretary of the Treasury Christopher G. Memminger.[54]

In 1861 the Confederacy levied a war tax on the states that the states generally assumed in order to ease the war burden for the people. To determine the amount, the states had to make an assessment by counties. The law gave the state a discount of ten percent if paid by 1 April 1862. Alabama's assessments were not completed on time, but in March 1862 Shorter made an agreement with Memminger for Alabama to pay the Confederacy $2 million. The agreement gave the Confederacy its tax money on time and allowed the state to receive its ten-percent discount. If the amount was not correct, it was agreed that adjustment would be made when the assessments were completed. To secure the $2 million, Shorter borrowed $1.7 million from Alabama banks and collected $300,000 from the Mobile and Ohio Railroad on a loan due the state. When the final settlement was made, Alabama owed the Confederacy another $100,000.[55]

Alabama met its debts abroad during the Shorter administration. To keep the state's credit good abroad, the governor sent $155,000 in specie through the blockade as interest on state bonds held by British investors. This was done with the permission of the Federal blockading squadron off Mobile, which allowed a British ship to pick up the money. However, the United States decided to make an issue of the matter with Great Britain and, because of that pressure, the British dismissed their consul in Mobile through whom Shorter had made the arrangements. This incident became a part of the larger controversy over accreditation of British consuls in the Confederacy—a controversy that ended in the expulsion of all in late 1863.[56]

As the war continued, financing became a serious problem. Neither the governor nor the Alabama legislature fully grasped the need to raise ad-

---

[54]Shorter to Arthur F. Hopkins, 5, 14 December 1861, 10 November 1862; Shorter to Hon. Wade Keyes, 26 October 1863; Shorter to Dr. C. J. Clark, 5 December 1861; *Acts of Alabama* (Called and Second Regular Annual Session, 1862), 202-203, approved by Governor Shorter 1 December 1862; F. A. Bates to Shorter, 26 July, 18 August 1862.

[55]Governor's Message, in *Journal of the Senate* (Called and Second Regular Annual Session, 1862), 75; Ibid. (Called and Third Regular Annual Session, 1863), 78; Shorter to Secretary Memminger, 14 May 1862.

[56]Troy *Southern Advertiser,* 3 April 1862; Frank L. Owsley, *King Cotton Diplomacy: Foreign Relations of the Confederate States of America* (Chicago, 1931) 476-77.

ditional taxes to pay for the war. Alabama, like the Confederacy and other
state governments, finally resorted to the almost unrestricted issuance of
paper currency, which contributed to runaway inflation. Inflation, in time,
brought financial collapse and this was a major cause of defeat. Although
the Alabama legislature authorized the issuance of paper money in 1861,
neither Shorter nor his predecessor, Governor Moore, resorted to this until
the former faced the almost impossible task of raising two million dollars
for indigent families in November 1862. At that time the state began issuing paper money in large amounts. Under the policy of forcing the banks
to suspend specie payments, all coins disappeared and were replaced by
change bills or "shin-plasters" issued by corporations, companies, or individuals. Shorter told the legislative session of November 1862 that the
privately issued change bills had become a public nuisance and requested
"some kind of paper currency to meet the demands of commerce to be issued by the state or banking corporations." The legislature decided that
the bills would be issued by the state, and the governor was authorized to
have "lithographed or engraved $2 million of treasury notes," later raised
in the same session to $3.5 million. The state was on its way, practically
overnight, to financing the war by printing its own paper money. Soon, the
money was rolling off the printing presses of James T. Patterson and Company of Columbia, South Carolina. Nevertheless, one student of Alabama
history concluded that "as basically unsound as the paper money policy of
Alabama was, the $7,542,680.00 issued in change bills and Treasury notes
was a paltry sum compared to the hundreds of millions emitted by the Confederate government." As financing the war became more demanding,
Watts issued more paper money in eighteen months than Shorter did in two
years.[57]

A problem that continued to plague the Confederacy was desertion. By
November 1862 it reached such huge proportions that President Davis, in
a circular letter to all Confederate governors, called upon them to aid the
Confederacy in returning deserters. Shorter gave one of the most vigorous
responses, calling upon all Alabamians to "give no shelter to deserters"
but to "drive them by the withering punishment of public scorn to their
proper places." He further asked that all give "aid to the proper officers

---

[57]Governor's Message, *Journal of the Senate* (Called and Second Regular Annual Session, 1862), 83; Milo B. Howard, "Alabama State Currency, 1861-1865," *Alabama Historical Quarterly* 25 (Spring-Summer 1963): 70-81, 82.

in arresting and coercing those who yield to no gentler means. It may be a disagreeable task, but the evil is great and ruinous to our country's cause, and it is part of the patriot now to shrink from no task, however disagreeable or dangerous."[58]

Shorter supported the controversial Gideon Pillow, who in 1863 was twice placed in charge of conscription in Alabama, Mississippi, and Tennessee, superseding the Richmond Bureau with a military plan of conscription supported by Generals Braxton Bragg and Joseph E. Johnston. His goal was to force deserters and absentees back into the Army of Tennessee and the Army of Mississippi. Pillow, whose headquarters for a time was in Huntsville, estimated that "from 8,000 to 10,000 deserters and Tory conscripts" were hiding in the mountains of Alabama. Many, he said, had deserted up to three and sometimes four times and were "as vicious as 'copperheads.' They have killed a number of my officers." Shorter wrote the secretary of war that the cause was lost unless the system was made to work and that he was sure that Pillow could "clear the country of stragglers, deserters, and conscripts" where the Conscription Bureau in Richmond had failed. Pillow was efficient at getting conscripts back in the army, but nobody could make them stay. Shorter, like Governor Watts at a later and more serious time, believed that the answer to desertion was to give the states and military commanders more control over conscription. After experimenting with Pillow, however, the Richmond authorities decided the Richmond Bureau could best handle the situation. The increase in desertions, however, caused the Confederacy to depend even more heavily on local authorities for the return of the deserters.

The second great wave of desertion followed Confederate defeats at Gettysburg and Vicksburg in the summer of 1863. The number of Tories and deserters in northern Alabama and the southeastern Alabama Wiregrass country increased precipitously. Alabama's problem with deserters seemed to be larger than that of any other Confederate state. By Shorter's second year in office, thousands of men had deserted the Confederate army and were hiding out in the sparsely settled Wiregrass or the hills of north Alabama. In July 1863 one estimate placed 8,000 in the hills alone. Because of his background as a secessionist, Shorter had little influence with

---

[58]Jefferson Davis to Shorter, 26 November 1862, in *OR,* ser. 4, vol. 2, 211; Shorter's Proclamation in Moore, *Rebellion Record* 6, Document 84.

these people. He tried to reach them through those loyal Confederates who had opposed secession until the die was cast. In northern Alabama he worked with Robert Jemison of Tuscaloosa, who became his aide for all northwest Alabama, and through Robert Patton of Florence, later governor. He also sent the personable James H. Clanton, who had opposed secession, to the Wiregrass to persuade deserters to join the army. Shorter's brother, ex-Congressman Eli Shorter, became his aide in southeast Alabama. He sent his brother to Richmond to persuade Jefferson Davis to allow Clanton to enlist deserters and conscripts into a special army to defend the Gulf Coast. In effect, this meant the suspension of conscription by the Richmond Bureau in that area. Clanton also visited Richmond. Shorter brought pressure on Davis through Senator C. C. Clay and others before the president finally acquiesced. The ploy was successful in getting a considerable number of absentees and deserters into Clanton's army, since they could stay close to home. However, it failed to make good Confederate soldiers out of them, and some later mutinied.[59]

Serious disorders were caused by bands of deserters who pillaged their neighbors. In the last year of his administration, Shorter faced problems that Watts would face throughout his governorship. The executive office received letters telling of the depredation by deserters and ruffians in nearly every county in the mountainous region south of the Tennessee Valley and the sparsely settled Wiregrass region. The letters from St. Clair County revealed conditions that were typical for the entire northern Alabama area. In July 1863, Shorter received a letter from a surgeon of the Ninth Alabama battalion. In writing for his men, he said that many of them had received by letter "the painful intelligence from home of their wives being outrage[d] and insulted, their meat and meal stolen from them—their last mouthful to eat taken by deserters." The letter asked Shorter to bring the

---

[59]Gideon J. Pillow to Col. Benjamin S. Ewell, *OR*, ser. 4, vol. 2, 680; Shorter to Jefferson Davis, 10 January 1863, in *OR*, ser. 1, vol. 15, 939-40; Shorter to Sec. of War Seddon, 14 January, 13 August 1863; Montgomery *Weekly Advertiser*, 4 February, 13 May 1863. In the fall of 1863 a detachment of troops in General James H. Clanton's army at Pollard mutinied. Many of them had been deserters from the Confederate army before they joined Clanton, and all of them were members of a peace society in which they had taken an oath to no longer fight against the United States. Some seventy of them were sent to Mobile for trial. General Bragg and others blamed the mutiny on Clanton. Shorter and later Watts defended Clanton, but his army was broken up and his troops sent elsewhere. Clanton was then given command of a small band of cavalry and sent to north Alabama.

offenders to trial and hinted that the men did not know how long they could stay at their posts unless their wives and children were protected. At about the same time Lieutenant Colonel Bush Jones, commander of the battalion, wrote the governor that about fifty of his unit had deserted, motivated by letters received from home about conditions in St. Clair County. The commander further stated that the county was infested by a band of traitors and deserters

> who are pillaging, robbing, harassing and intimidating the families of loyal citizens. . . . They are committing every kind of outrage that could be committed by a lawless band of robbers and enemies. They not only maltreat and impoverish the soldiers' families but they threaten the lives of and lie in wait for those who are sent to arrest them. So great many are the outrages committed by them that many families have fled for protection. . . . In many portions of the country it is unsafe for a soldier loyal to the Confederacy to return to his home, sick or wounded.

Jones's letter stated that cavalry sent to arrest deserters could not operate in counties like St. Clair because of the mountains covered by heavy underbrush, where a man on foot had every advantage over a mounted one. Furthermore, he said, "The cavalry have consumed the provisions of the good people without even intimidating the bad, thereby aggravating the distress."[60]

Desertion and disorders became so overwhelming in northern and southeastern Alabama that the state could not handle the situation. Shorter opened all jails in the state for the detention of deserters as they were being carried back to their posts. When the jailer in DeKalb County refused to accept deserters, Shorter told the sheriff of the county to use the jail for this purpose. The governor placed all the moral force of his office against desertion, telling his aides-de-camp throughout the state to use the combined forces of the militia and volunteers to arrest local bands of deserters. However, the state was fighting a losing battle from the start. Good men may have felt justified in deserting when their families were in danger but, once they deserted, they were forced to go underground and became outlaws themselves—ever hiding from the law. News of deserters in St. Clair and surrounding counties (the most often mentioned were Cherokee,

[60]E. J. Riskrey and others to Shorter, 18 July 1863; Lieut. Col. Bush Jones to Shorter, 16 July 1863.

DeKalb, Jackson and Marshall counties) spread far and wide. Captain John A. Averett, Jr., whose company was stationed in North Carolina, wrote the governor asking to have his company transferred back to Alabama where he and his men would be closer to their families in St. Clair. Shorter replied that he had organized a local force in the county under the direction of his aide-de-camp, Arthur C. Beard, "for protection to the families desired by the men of your command." The governor told Averett that since his company was in the Confederate service it would be impossible to obtain orders for its removal to Alabama. "Even though detached, I think you need be under no apprehension as to future depredation upon the families of your command," Shorter said. The governor was overly optimistic. Beard's local force was unable to bring the deserters under control, and they defeated the cavalry sent against them from the conscript camp at Talladega.[61]

Deserters were often stronger than any force the state sent against them. In June 1863 Shorter sent Captain Thomas Armstrong, commander of a militia unit, the Henry County Rebels, and some men from General Clanton's brigade to capture deserters in Henry and Dale counties—where about a dozen of them were hiding in the Pea River swamps. Armstrong and his men captured six deserters and one conscript and brought them back to camp. The deserters were then placed under a guard of six men and sent to the jail in Abbeville in Henry County. When they were within twenty miles of the jail, the group was attacked by about thirty deserters who killed, or seriously wounded, one of the guards and rescued their fellows. After this incident, a whole company of troops chased after the deserters, but they faded into the swamps and could not be found. In desperation, Captain Armstrong arrested two old men and charged them with treason for aiding and abetting the deserters, but Shorter ordered the old men released unless Armstrong had sworn evidence against them that could hold up in court.[62]

---

[61]Shorter to Capt. John A. Averett Jr., 25 March 1863; Shorter to Col. Arthur C. Beard, 15 May 1863; Shorter to Gen. Braxton Bragg, 24 July 1863.

[62]Shorter to Capt. Thomas Armstrong, 7 July 1863; Armstrong to Shorter, 2 July 1863. Shorter said there was a difference between arresting deserters and arresting traitors. "As the state is not under martial law and civil process is not suspended," he said, "I have given no orders to arrest Tories. Such measures are useless unless there is evidence to sustain the charge of treason." He thought the "arrest on the charge of treason an authority

Shorter finally wrote an apologetic letter to General Bragg in Tennessee asking for help from his army in controlling deserters. Shorter told him that desertion was really a military matter, but that disorders among the people caused by deserters fell under civil law and the state was responsible. The state, however, "is left powerless to enforce the laws against armed combinations in the sparsely settled districts" of Alabama. Enumerating all the consequences of nonenforcement, he observed, "How the law can be enforced in counties such as St. Clair, I must confess passes my comprehension." He thought one of the most important consequences would be that "good men willing to serve their country, will hesitate to leave their families to the tender mercies of these bandits."[63]

Letters reached the executive office complaining that the cavalry sent out to arrest deserters was dissolute. One letter, signed by eight Barbour countians of the Fifty-fourth Alabama Regiment, reminded Shorter that he was also from Barbour County. They wanted to know if he was responsible for the cavalry who were "prowling through our county on pretense of getting deserters" but who were actually "mistreating our aged fathers, mothers," and other citizens. They further charged that "soldiers' families are insulted, there [sic] stock killed and there [sic] houses plundered" by the cavalry.[64]

The absence of an adequate militia became a major problem. The buildup of the Confederate armies caused the state to be drained of its manpower, and its militia gradually faded away. Troops were available for the Virginia and Tennessee fronts but, the governor realized in early 1862, state forces to keep order and to defend the state were very scarce. The state militia, which was nurtured during the days before removal of the Indians, was neglected in the immediate period before the war, especially in the rural areas. In March 1862, when an attack on Mobile by the Federal fleet seemed imminent, Shorter called out the militia from eighteen counties in

---

which the constitution and the laws have not placed in my hands." Watts took the same position in the case of David C. Humphries, who was arrested in Huntsville for making a "treasonable address" against the Confederacy and sent to Watts in Montgomery. After studying the case, Watts said that although the address was objectionable, he saw nothing in it which would authorize him to hold Humphries in custody. See Proclamation of Watts, 13 December 1864.

[63]Shorter to Gen. Braxton Bragg, 29 July 1863.

[64]B. F. Holmes and others to Shorter, 20 July 1863.

southwest Alabama and on the rivers above Mobile. The militia, as a whole, failed to respond and the governor called for it a second time before concluding that the Confederate army had absorbed most of its men. Early in the war the Confederate army offered excitement and glory; the militia, by comparison, seemed drab. Walter L. Fleming declared in *Civil War and Reconstruction in Alabama* that "many of the militia regiments were so depleted they could not have mustered a dozen men." This was even before passage of the Conscription Act in April 1862, which subjected most of those left in the militia to conscription. The governor realized that the only hope of salvaging the state force was by extending the age limits. The governor called on the entire white male population between the ages of sixteen and sixty, and who were not subject to the draft, to organize themselves into volunteer units to be called the State Guard. The response, as he later said, "was not prompt."[65]

In October 1862 Shorter called a special session of the legislature and recommended that the militia be reorganized so as to "embrace all ablebodied citizens of the state above the age of sixteen and under the age of sixty years" not subject to the draft. However, the legislature failed to act because of (1) the scarcity of manpower, (2) the unwillingness of many to do state service, and (3) the likelihood that a reorganized militia might be absorbed into the Confederate army. Shorter declared that the failure bordered on criminal negligence. Reflecting the feeling that defense was a priority of the Confederate government, the legislature passed a law, repealed several sessions later, specifying that militia officers, justices of the peace, and notaries public were subject to conscription. This further weakened the militia. Shorter did not advocate this law, but was reluctant to veto it.[66]

After legislative adjournment, Shorter again asked the people to form volunteer companies, but the response was disappointing. In truth, there was very little suitable manpower left for the militia. The best organized militia was in Mobile and the surrounding area, home of Thomas J. Butler, who was major general of the militia. The need for a strong militia became greater in northern Alabama and the Wiregrass country because of the accumulation of stragglers and deserters in those areas.

---

[65]Governor's Proclamation Book, 6 March, 12 May 1862; Fleming, *Alabama,* 89-90.

[66]Governor's Message in *Journal of the Senate* (Called and Second Regular Annual Session, 1862), 19; Fleming, *Alabama,* 89-90.

As Confederate armies were destroyed, the need for a strong militia became more obvious. Although this was first recognized as a potential problem by Governor Moore, the need to strengthen the militia became even more crucial under Shorter and reached crisis proportions under Governor Watts. After July 1863 Lee's retreat from Gettysburg—and especially the fall of Vicksburg—lowered morale at home and in the Confederate army. Thousands of disgruntled Alabama soldiers paroled at Vicksburg made their way across Mississippi to their homes in Alabama. Despondency and desertion increased everywhere. One of the few bright spots in that year was the capture of Abel D. Streight's raiders by Nathan Bedford Forrest's cavalry in north Alabama. Rumors reached Governor Shorter that other raiders were being trained to strike at Montgomery and Selma from north Alabama, and he called on Joseph E. Johnston, commander of the Department of the West, for troops to defend the state. Johnston advised him to call up the militia, but the governor replied that the militia was powerless. He added that in his recent attempts to force those having substitutes and others into the militia, most of them sought ''pretexts in every manner to avoid duty, even to a resort to a *habeas corpus* before ignorant justices of the peace, who have no jurisdiction of their cases.''[67]

In 1863 the reorganization of the militia became crucial both to quell disorders at home and to help defend the state as the army of the enemy moved closer. Shorter contemplated calling back into session the same legislature which failed to create an effective militia in October 1862. However, he finally decided to await the election of August 1863, thinking that a legislature elected by the people in the midst of a crisis on the home and war fronts would surely face up to the situation. He was mistaken. The people voted him out of office by an overwhelming margin and sent to Montgomery a legislature made up of mostly obscure men who were quite inclined to sue for peace and were ready to sabotage the war efforts of the Alabama governors. In July 1863, Shorter called the yet-to-be-elected legislature into session for 17 August 1863, the first day he could call the body into session under the 1861 constitution. The timing of the governor indicates that he was unaware of the overwhelming defeat he would soon suffer or the mood of the electorate with regard to the war. The August

---

[67]Shorter to Joseph Johnston, 28 July, 4 August 1863, in *OR,* vol. 24, pt. 3, 1035; Johnston to Shorter, 2 August 1863, ibid., vol. 26, pt. 2, 136; Shorter to Johnston, 4 August 1863, ibid., 139-40.

1863 legislature would never support the executive in a strong prosecution of the war, as Shorter and then Thomas H. Watts would discover.[68]

During this time Shorter wrote, "I await with anxiety the assemblage of the state legislature . . . for upon its prompt and patriotic action will depend all further efficiency of the state militia." In his address to the legislature he urged that all white males between the ages of sixteen and sixty, including those having substitutes, all aliens living in the state, and all those who, for various reasons, were not in the Confederate army, be drafted into a militia force to protect the state and enforce the law against stragglers and deserters. He appealed to the legislature and the people not to give way to "alarm and trepidation," but to "nerve their resolution for an undying resistance against that abolition despotism which has decreed the emancipation of the slaves, the confiscation of lands, and the subjugation of the free inhabitants of these sovereign states and their heirs forever." In conclusion, he said that "if we do our part, God in his just providence will not permit such an awful calamity."[69]

Debate in the legislature centered around opposition to placing the young and the old in uniform. Some argued that boys under eighteen and men over forty-five would not make good soldiers and that their services were required at home to support the women and children and provide food for the army. Legislators also expressed fear of an "all absorbing Confederate army," and a later session of this same legislature actually passed a law providing that no part of the militia could be commanded by a Confederate officer. To meet the various objections, those who supported a reorganization of the militia finally came up with a class-one and class-two militia system that, on its face, was absurd and certainly cumbersome. Boys between sixteen and seventeen and men between forty-five and sixty were placed in class one, known as the county reserve. The law provided that county reserves were only liable for service in their respective counties,

---

[68]Shorter to Messers. A. C. Beard, W. D. Chadick, J. B. Wisdom and Nicholas Davis, 16 May 1863. On 13 May these gentlemen had sent Shorter a petition urging him to call the old legislature back into session. In his answer of 16 May, Shorter argues the case for waiting for the new legislature which, chosen under the pressure of current events, "would be better fitted to adopt the measures necessary for the crisis."

[69]Governor's Message in *Journal of the Senate* (Called and Third Annual Regular Session, 1863), 8-17; Shorter to Braxton Bragg, 24 July 1863; Shorter to Joseph E. Johnston, 4 August 1863.

which made them useless in organized defense, but kept them on the farms where they could grow food for the home front and the army and, presumably, keep order. The class two, or the state reserves, would consist of all white males between seventeen and forty-five years of age not in the Confederate army. This group was limited to a few thousand exempts, detailed, and substitute men. Shorter signed the bill because, as he said, "It fails to come up to the emergency but it was the best I could get." The law would give Governor Watts, Shorter's successor, much trouble as the unorganized militia again became the subject of controversy. Though totally inadequate, the two-class plan remained, with minor amendments, the militia law for the remainder of the war. This arrangement meant that much of the remaining Alabama manpower could not be used to defend the state in the last crucial years of the war.[70]

Although one Civil War scholar interpreted Governor Shorter's concern about the militia as a selfish attempt to build a state army at the expense of the Confederate army, Confederate officials demanded a strong militia. They called on Shorter repeatedly to use the militia to defend positions or to bolster Confederate forces. Jefferson Davis, complaining about the lack of Confederate forces at Mobile, told Shorter to organize the militia to defend that city. After the Battle of Shiloh, Davis telegraphed Shorter and four other Southern governors: "The necessity is imminent; the case of vital importance; send forward to Corinth all the armed men you can furnish." In the fall of 1863, as Federal forces moved toward Atlanta, Davis sent Colonel James Chesnut to visit Governors Shorter and Brown to urge the sending of "reinforcements—local defense men or militia—to the aid of Genls. Bragg and Buckner against whom the enemy is moving in force. Northern Georgia and Alabama can be best defended by increasing the army in East Tennessee," Davis said.[71]

As the election of August 1863 approached, Confederate Attorney General Thomas H. Watts wrote to a friend saying that although he would not campaign, he would accept the governorship of Alabama "if called by

---

[70]*Acts of the Called and Third Regular Annual Session of the General Assembly of Alabama, 1863,* 3-11; Shorter to Dabney H. Maury, 9 September 1863; *Montgomery Weekly Advertiser,* 19, 29 October 1863.

[71]See Owsley, *State Rights,* 33; Davis to Shorter, 10 April 1862, in Rowland, *Davis Letters,* 5:230; Davis to Col. James Chesnut, ibid., 6:19. In the latter Davis urges Chesnut to visit Shorter in the interest of having militia sent to east Tennessee.

the people." Watts was already in a high Confederate position and it was obvious that he wished to be governor. Although Shorter became the scapegoat for almost every problem brought by a bloody civil war, he said that he did not "feel at liberty to decline serving the state for a second term, according to past usage." If he stepped aside under pressure, his enemies would say that the charges were true. He decided to fight for his convictions. In an address to the people he stated his intention to run again and reviewed his administration. He said also that he was aware of "complaints against my administration, but believing them to be undeserved, I was willing to bear them with resignation for the good of the state, trusting that time would disclose my record and vindicate my course." He spoke of the burdens of the governor's office in wartime and of "an inward approval, which the popular verdict shall neither give nor take away."[72]

The people voted Shorter out of office by an overwhelming majority of 28,221 for Watts to 9,664 for Shorter, with 1,471 votes going to a third candidate, James Dowdell. Watts's majority was about three to one. Shorter carried only four northern Alabama counties, and was beaten in his own county of Barbour by almost 400 votes. In 1861 he had been elected by heavy majorities in northern and eastern Alabama; in 1863, he lost these areas and the rest of the state. The month before, Shorter wrote Braxton Bragg that he was "afraid our reverses in the west will affect our election." Of the effect of the fall of Vicksburg there can be no doubt, but a long, hard, self-sacrificing war had the most telling effect.[73]

The crushing defeat of Shorter in August 1863 was the result of many factors. The stronghold of the Democratic party in Alabama was always in the northern part of the state. After April 1862 that area was decimated by the war. The Federals adopted the "scorched earth" policy of William Tecumseh Sherman and ground the population under foot. The rigors of civil war in the area and Shorter's inability to drive out the enemy turned his Democratic constituency against him. The marriage had always been shaky. In 1861, Shorter, the ardent secessionist, had been elected governor by the most reluctant secessionists in the state because of the strength of the Democratic party in that area.

---

[72]Shorter, "Address to the People" in Montgomery *Weekly Advertiser*, 15 July 1863.

[73]Shorter to Braxton Bragg, 24 July 1863. For election returns by counties, see *Journal of the House of Representatives* (Called and Third Regular Annual Session, 1863) 110-11.

Shorter's acquiescence in the troop consolidation efforts by the Confederates at strategic points, which allowed the enemy to maintain itself in northern Alabama, had aroused great hostility against him. In June 1863, Thomas J. Foster, Confederate congressman from northern Alabama, reproached Shorter for not driving the enemy out. In late 1862 the legislature had appropriated one million dollars for that purpose. Shorter, in answering Foster, said, "Individual, local, and sectional interests—however great and important—must be held subordinate to the grand idea of Confederate success. If the Confederacy fails, all is lost." Yet Shorter, in writing the Confederate secretary of war about the neglect of Alabama, could also earnestly plead Alabama's cause. Shorter told the congressman that he had no troops capable of driving the enemy out and that, even with troops, he had no arms to give them. He said that the contracts calling for delivery of 8,000 Mississippi rifles to the state by 1 May 1863 had not produced a single gun. In closing, Shorter asked Foster to present him with concrete plans on how to drive the enemy out. He asked the congressman to help organize the State Guard in the area because there was little response to his proclamation urging its formation.[74]

The reversal, as indicated by the 1863 election, against Shorter, who was an able and energetic war governor, can only be interpreted as a protest against the secessionists of 1861, their hard and apparently unsuccessful war, and against the Democratic party, which the people held responsible for their woes.

Historians of the Whig party have pointed out that the Whigs made significant gains in 1863 in Alabama and other Confederate states. This was because they were fortunate to be the "outs" in a war situation that had become deplorable and intolerable. The Whigs, of course, profited immeasurably because of their reluctance to break up the old Union. The "fire-eaters" were all in the Democratic party. Peace and restoration were shown to be the issue in 1863 because eighteen months after assuming office, Thomas Watts, the old Whig who turned out to be "a war man all over," was in as much political trouble as Shorter. Watts had no chance of re-election, and powerful peace forces were looking elsewhere for their leader.

---

[74]McMillan, *Alabama Confederate Reader,* 180-81; John Brawner Robbins, *Confederate Nationalism: Politics and Government in the Confederate South, 1861-1865* (Ph.D. dissertation, Rice University, 1964) 209; Fleming, *Alabama,* 162-63; Thomas J. Foster to Shorter, 3 June 1863; Shorter to Foster, 11 June 1863.

Because the Whigs had been more conservative on the issue of secession, the electorate thought they would be in a much stronger position to make peace than the Democrats. Thousands of Alabamians seeking peace in 1863 flocked to Watts's camp. He did not tell them that he was not a "reconstructionist"—that is, not until after the election, when he already had their votes. This colossal error, occurring in the midst of a great civil war, is the best evidence yet that the Confederacy made a huge mistake when it allowed the South's two-party system to die during the war. The failure to hold conventions, debate the issues, and let the people know each candidate's stand brought about this farcical, yet serious, episode. A strong two-party system would have strengthened Shorter but, instead, he stood alone and was all but helpless in the face of criticism that came from all directions. A closely knit party to answer criticisms and share the blame would have strengthened and comforted him. Politicians in the North enjoyed this strength, but it was denied to their Southern counterparts.[75]

In summary, John Gill Shorter was a statesman who made difficult decisions while ignoring political expediency. Perhaps he possessed too much of that "inward approval" of which he spoke. A less self-righteous individual might have made a better politician, but historians who are knowledgeable of his administration have generally praised him. Frank Vandiver wrote in *Ploughshares into Swords,* "The Confederacy possessed too few men of the quality of Shorter." In 1872, the year of Shorter's death, historian William Garrett declared, "In justice to Gov. Shorter, it may be said that it was utterly impossible for any man to fulfill the public expectations, and to satisfy all complaints during the war. . . . The sentence against him," Garrett continued, "was harsh indeed, and it is believed that it was uncalled for and unauthorized on the principle of justice." In most of the letters he wrote after his defeat, the governor showed no bitterness. In a letter to Lieutenant General W. T. Hardee on 8 September 1863, he wrote that he had been "stricken down for holding up the state to its high resolves and crowding the people to the performance of their duty."[76]

---

[75]Thomas B. Alexander, "Persistent Whiggery in Alabama and the Lower South, 1860-1867," *Alabama Review* 12 (January 1959): 35-52; McKitrick, "Party Politics and the Union and Confederate War Efforts," in *The American Party System: Stages of Political Development,* ed. William Nisbet Chambers and Walter Dean Burnham (New York, 1967) 117-51.

[76]Frank E. Vandiver, *Ploughshares into Swords: Josiah Gorgas and Confederate Ord-*

Shorter cooperated gracefully with Watts on his inauguration day and then retired to Eufaula for the few remaining years of his life. He continued his law practice and appeared briefly at Conservative Reconstruction meetings in Montgomery at the end of the war. Although some historians contradict this, there is no evidence that Shorter was arrested and imprisoned by Federal authorities.[77] Shorter's health had always been delicate and in January 1872 he caught a severe cold and developed tuberculosis. On 29 May of that year he died whispering the words of the old hymn "To Canaan's fair and happy land, where my possessions lie," which he ended with "I want to be off."[78] In Shorter's eulogy, General Alpheus Baker said, "Men die daily, but few such men as John Gill Shorter die in a cycle of years, because there are few such men to die."[79]

---

nance (Austin, 1952) 73; Garrett, *Reminiscences,* 722; Shorter to General Hardee, 8 September 1863.

[77]Fleming, *Alabama,* 262; Moore, *History of Alabama,* 460. Both Fleming and Moore say he was imprisoned, but neither cites a source. *OR* contains an account of the imprisonment of Andrew Barry Moore and the arrest and detention of Governor Watts, but no evidence of even the arrest of Shorter.

[78]*The Death Bed of Ex-Governor John Gill Shorter* (Philadelphia, n.d.) 1-12.

[79]Eufaula *Daily Times,* 11 May 1872.

Chapter III

THOMAS HILL WATTS:
"A War Man All Over"

Thomas Hill Watts took the oath of office as governor of Alabama in December 1863 with an established and noteworthy record as lawyer-planter, legislator, and Confederate cabinet member. He was born in the Alabama Territory on 3 January 1819, the year the state entered the Union, and grew to manhood in an area, now Butler County, that had only recently been ceded by the Creek Indians. In 1818 his father, John Hughes Watts, and mother, Prudence Hill, moved from Georgia seeking the better lands of the frontier. Thomas was the oldest of twelve children born to them.[1]

Thomas showed an early aptitude for books. At the age of sixteen, his father sent him to Airy Mount Academy in Dallas County where the principal, James A. McLean of Edinburgh, Scotland, recognized his natural ability and prepared him for college. His father had quite a large family by 1836 and could not educate all of his children, but Thomas asked for a col-

---

[1]Hallie Farmer, "Thomas H. Watts" in Dumas Malone, ed., *Dictionary of American Biography* (New York, 1936) 10:557; Garrett, *Reminiscences*, 723-25; Brewer, *Alabama*, 460-61.

lege education instead of part of his father's estate. They entered a verbal
agreement to this effect and records show that at his father's death in 1861
Watts had the probate court honor this agreement.[2]

In 1836 he left for the University of Virginia and graduated with hon-
ors four years later. He came home in July 1840, when the Whig "log
cabin" campaign was at its height, and affiliated with that party. The next
year, after passing the bar examination, he began the practice of law at
Greenville where he soon acquired a reputation as a promising young lawyer. In 1842, 1843, and 1845 he represented Butler County in the lower
house of the state legislature and in the latter year he worked hard to change
the capital to Montgomery. During his legislative years he took a strong
stand against the practice of "treating" the electorate with liquor on the
hustings and helped to bring the practice under control. In January 1848
he moved his already lucrative law practice to Montgomery, the new capital, where he was joined by Thomas J. Judge and others. The prosperity
and growth of the firm was attested by the number of factorage houses in
New York and Boston that used it in their Alabama business in the 1850s.[3]
In the same decade Watts also became a planter. The census of 1860 shows
that he had 179 slaves on his Montgomery County plantation and produced
552 bales of cotton and 1,000 bushels of corn. He listed livestock valued
at $5,500.[4]

In the 1848 campaign Watts became a Taylor elector. In 1849 he represented Montgomery County in the lower house of the legislature, playing a leading role in maneuvers that tied up a Democrat-controlled House
so that a Democratic and perhaps extremist delegation could not be elected
to the Nashville Convention. Later an informal-but-unofficial session of
legislators compromised by sending an equal number of Democrats and
Whigs to Nashville.[5] Throughout the crisis of the Union in the 1850s, Watts
adopted a pro-Union stance, although later developments make the depth
of his convictions questionable. In 1853 the Whigs of Montgomery and

[2]*Representative Men of the South* (Philadelphia, 1880) 41.

[3]Lewis E. Antherton, "The Problem of Credit Rating in the Ante-bellum South," *Journal of Southern History* 12 (November 1946): 549.

[4]Manuscript Census of Alabama, 1860, Agricultural and Slave Schedules.

[5]Thornton, *Politics and Power,* 185.

Autauga counties elected Watts to the state senate where he initiated steps
that led to a geological survey of the state.

As the Whig party disintegrated in the middle part of the 1850s, Watts
found temporary refuge in the Know-Nothing party, which in 1855 nominated him as its candidate for Congress in the Montgomery district. He
lost to James F. Dowdell, the Democratic candidate, by a small margin.
On the eve of the Civil War, he was one of the acknowledged leaders of
those opposing the Democrats.

During the antebellum years Watts was described by one observer as
"large and stout, erect and a little more than six feet in height. He is affable and sociable and quite popular with all classes." Another account described him as "of strong and vigorous physical constitution, tall—six feet
two inches in his stocking feet—and proportioned accordingly." Others
spoke of his massive head, adorned by small gold-rimmed glasses. Some
of his friends called him "Big Tom" Watts.[6]

Despite his background as a Unionist, Watts played a key role in the
secession of Alabama in January 1861. Only months before he had campaigned for John Bell, believing that the Constitutional Unionist candidate
could save the Union. Late in the campaign, however, when Lincoln's
election seemed likely, Watts declared that he would advocate secession
if Lincoln were elected. After Lincoln's election he asserted that he had
always recognized the right of a "sovereign state" to secede to protect its
interest. He said that secession should be based on the "higher ground"
of the "sovereign rights" of a state rather than "constitutional rights";
pointing out that sovereign and independent states had formed the Union,
he argued that these same states could withdraw from it and form another.
Debating against the cooperationists, Watts declared that each state had
entered the Union separately, that was the only way to leave it. He said
that as long as Alabama remained in the Union, any meeting of Southern
states was unconstitutional and treasonable.[7]

---

[6]Brewer, *Alabama,* 460; *Representative Men,* 41; Knapp, "William Phineas Browne,"
Alabama Review 3 (April, 1950): 114.

[7]Watts to S. J. Bolling and L. D. Steele, 10 November 1860, is an excellent exposition
of why Watts thought the time had come for secession. See Montgomery *Weekly Post,* 14
November 1860; Jeane Lynch, "Thomas Hill Watts: War Governor of Alabama, 1863-
1865" (Master's thesis, Auburn University, 1957) 9.

In the election for the convention Watts and William L. Yancey both ran as secessionists from Montgomery County and Watts actually got more votes than Yancey. During the convention meeting the two men entered the hall walking "arm in arm," a foreboding sign indeed to the cooperationists, one of whom wrote that "Watts' defection will do ten times the mischief" it would have done if he had supported John C. Breckinridge for president.[8]

In the convention, Watts became chairman of the Judiciary Committee and one of the secession leaders. However, he did try to temper some of the rashness of the extreme secessionist leaders led by Yancey. Debate over immediate secession became very bitter. The cooperationists' efforts to block immediate secession brought a cry of "treason against Alabama" from Yancey. The cooperationists in turn challenged Yancey to lead the secessionists to the hills of northern Alabama where a decision might be left to guns. At this point Watts tried to pour oil on troubled waters by rebuking Yancey. He supported all of the measures of the immediate secessionists, however, including the seizure of federal forts in Alabama and the sending of Alabama troops to Pensacola, both of which occurred before the passage of the ordinance of secession. Believing that war with the Union was inevitable, he introduced an ordinance in the convention for the confiscation of all enemy property in Alabama.[9]

After the ordinance of secession was adopted (Watts was one of the signers), the convention proceeded to exclude leading members of the secession convention from the Confederate meeting. This was accomplished by not voting for them as members of the Confederate Convention, which became the Provisional Congress. This effort to placate the cooperationists prevented Watts and Yancey from taking part in the formation of the new government for the Confederacy. However, Watts was appointed by Governor Moore to the committee to meet president-elect Jefferson Davis at West Point, Georgia, on the state's border, and escort him to Montgomery. At that time and at subsequent socials hosted by the Wattses during the Montgomery phase of the Confederacy, Davis formed a high opinion of Watts, and when the permanent Confederate constitution

---

[8]Jeremiah Clemens to Senator J. J. Crittenden in McMillan, *Alabama Confederate Reader*, 13-15.

[9]Smith, *Debates*, 52, 68-70, 175.

went into effect in early 1862, he asked him to be attorney general. Watts and his wife entertained lavishly during the Montgomery months of the Confederacy and Davis was a guest in their home on more than one occasion. Davis also learned of Watts's reputation as a lawyer and jurist while the Confederacy was in Montgomery.[10]

In June 1861 the Montgomery *Daily Post* nominated Watts as candidate for governor in the August elections, nominating conventions having been abandoned for the war. The *Post* said that he was a man whom all parties could support; thus party bickering would be eliminated. In this election five candidates were nominated by the newspapers, but all except Watts and Shorter withdrew. In July Watts also withdrew. This left only Shorter, a member of the Confederate Congress, as a declared candidate. The *Daily Post* concluded that Watts would serve if elected and reentered his name at the head of its columns. Editorially the *Post* became extremely critical of Shorter for seeking office while holding a seat in the Congress. Five days before the election, Watts stated that an office tendered him as a "freewill offering from the people" would be accepted. In the absence of nominating conventions and with what amounted to double-talk by the friends of the candidates, there was great confusion. Shorter was elected but the strong showing by Watts under the circumstances indicated the high regard the people had for him. Watts carried twenty-four counties (mostly in central and southern Alabama) and Shorter twenty-seven (mostly in northern and eastern Alabama). Thus despite all admonitions to dissolve the parties, the people voted according to established geographical alliances, upholding old party affiliations.[11]

Watts was defeated for governor but was nominated in the legislature for a seat in the Confederate Senate. After ten ballots, C. C. Clay won by a vote of sixty-six to fifty-three, partially because Clay was from northern Alabama, a section that always elected one of the senators.[12] Watts then

---

[10]Moore, *History of Alabama,* 423; Lynch, "Watts," 11. For Watts's social life during these years, see Mrs. Thomas Hill Watts (born Eliza Allen) in Watts folder. Library, ADAH. Eliza Allen Watts died in 1873, and in 1875 Watts married Mrs. E. C. Jackson, the widow of his former law partner, J. F. Jackson.

[11]McMillan, *Alabama Confederate Reader,* 233; Lynch, "Watts," 12-14; "Election Returns" in *Journal of the Second Called and First Regular Annual Session of the House of Representatives, 1861,* 117-18.

[12]Nuermberger, *The Clays of Alabama,* 189-90.

organized the Seventeenth Alabama Regiment, composed mainly of volunteers from central Alabama, and was elected its colonel. He served with the regiment at Pensacola and went with it to Corinth. Before the Battle of Shiloh, Watts heard that Davis had appointed him attorney general under the permanent constitution. He resigned his commission as colonel and left for Richmond the following day.

Watts reached Richmond and took the oath as attorney general on 9 April 1862. In *Jefferson Davis and His Cabinet*, Rembert Patrick described him at this time as "powerful of frame, with a massive head and features that bespoke a resolute character." Patrick added that "the Alabamian pleased the Richmond public from its first glimpse of him."[13] Watts was fortunate in having another competent Alabamian, assistant attorney general Wade Keyes, to accomplish the routine departmental work. Keyes, however, could not protect Watts from well-wishers and others from Alabama who came to Richmond. The attorney general found that his job was a taxing one. He wrote to Daniel S. Troy, his son-in-law in Alabama, that it would take "an animal with more heads and arms and voice" than a man had "to do all that the public expected of the attorney-general." In addition to the legitimate business, which was "sufficient to keep a pretty good worker busy," Watts said that he was forced to "entertain all Alabamians who ever knew or heard of me," attend to their business with the government, and visit their sick in the hospitals.[14] Despite this pressure, Watts ran an efficient office. When he arrived in Richmond, he paid a courtesy call on other departments. Observing a curt incivility that "a brief authority" had brought to clerks in other offices, he issued an order telling his clerks and ushers that "incivility even to a beggar" in his department would be the quickest way to get demoted. Watts was asked to interpret laws from all over the Confederacy but felt that his jurisdiction was limited to interpreting Confederate laws for the president and heads of departments. In eighteen months as attorney general, he wrote more than 100 opinions while carefully citing their precedents in legal history. His two predecessors had written only twenty.[15]

---

[13]Rembert W. Patrick, *Jefferson Davis and His Cabinet* (Baton Rouge, 1944) 304.

[14]Watts to Daniel S. Troy, 24 May 1862. Unless otherwise stated, all Watts letters cited are in the Watts Collection, ADAH.

[15]Patrick, *Davis and His Cabinet,* 304-305.

As attorney general, Watts apparently gave first priority to upholding the central government. His advocacy of a Confederate Supreme Court places him on the side of the centralists at this time. He overruled Judah P. Benjamin, his predecessor, when he declared that officers of state troops called into Confederate service should be appointed by the president because these troops were responsible to the president as their commander in chief. He assured Davis that the Conscription Act of 1862 was constitutional since the Confederate Congress had unrestricted power to provide for the national defense. In another opinion he ruled that foreigners who possess property in the Confederacy and who did not give evidence of returning to their native land were subject to conscription. Watts got along well with Davis and members of the cabinet with the possible exception of the secretaries of war. George W. Randolph once submitted an issue to Watts and then tried to place his own contrary interpretation on the law, but Davis ruled that after submitting the matter to Watts, Randolph must follow his advice. Some controversy between James A. Seddon and Watts also arose because Watts refused to withdraw the prosecution of an Alabama company for trading with the enemy. Although Watts was attorney general for only a year and a half, Rembert Patrick ranked him as one of the most important members of Davis's cabinet.[16] When Federal raiders reached the Richmond vicinity in the summer of 1863, the attorney general assumed command of a company of Confederate troops and defended the city.[17]

As the election of August 1863 approached in Alabama and his friends prepared to nominate him, Watts was torn between continuing to hold "the honorable and responsible position tendered me by the President" or seeking the highest office in his native state. In the end the governorship seemed more attractive, and he wrote that he would not "canvass or scramble" for the office but would "accept the governorship if the people so desired."[18]

In making this decision, Watts must have thought he could do a better job than Shorter, but he probably also was aware of the great discontent in Alabama with the party of secession and the war. Senator C. C. Clay's correspondents in Alabama kept him abreast of the situation and there is

---

[16]Ibid., 306, 366.

[17]Montgomery *Weekly Advertiser*, 29 July 1863.

[18]McMillan, *Alabama Confederate Reader*, 234; Montgomery *Weekly Mail*, 1 July 1863.

no indication that Watts was any less informed. Clay wrote his friend, Senator Louis T. Wigfall of Texas, that in Alabama, "You may look out for the Old Whigs and Douglasites taking possession of the Governorship, Cong. and Legis. There is a strong feeling of dissatisfaction with those in office . . . that threatens to throw us all out, especially those regarded as the President's special friends."[19]

In an effort to answer his critics, Shorter issued a circular to the press defending his administration. Watts's friends then issued a handbill attacking the governor because he had not driven the enemy out of northern Alabama despite the fact that the legislature had appropriated $1 million for its defense. They also charged that Shorter's efforts to furnish the families of soldiers with salt and cotton cards were insufficient. Consequently the poor could neither cure their meat nor card cotton or wool to clothe themselves and their children.[20]

As we have already seen, Watts defeated Shorter in the August 1863 gubernatorial election by a vote of about three to one. Once again he was a reluctant candidate. He wrote General Levi W. Lawler of Talladega that although he would not be an active candidate, "I cannot refuse to serve . . . my people in any position they choose to place me."[21] During the campaign he remained in Richmond. Watts carried every county in Alabama, except four in the northern part of the state, and even ran ahead of Shorter in his home county of Barbour.[22]

A report on the Alabama election sent to the Conscription Bureau in Richmond several days after it took place stated that "in this section of the state [the Talladega District] the elections have been generally carried by an opposition known as the 'Peace Party.' " They not only voted for Watts but in some counties "elected to the State Legislature and to other positions of public trust [men] who are not publicly known, or scarcely known

---

[19]Nuermberger, *The Clays of Alabama,* 224, quoting C. C. Clay.

[20]Shorter's Campaign Circular in Montgomery *Weekly Advertiser,* 8 July 1863; Handbill by "Friends of Watts" addressed "to the people of Alabama" in Watts Papers, ADAH. The flyer is not dated but contains an account of the Twenty-fifth Alabama's straw ballot favoring Watts, dated 18 July 1863. An account of the straw ballot appeared later in Alabama newspapers. See Selma *Reporter,* 24 July 1863.

[21]Watts to Levi Lawler in Montgomery *Weekly Advertiser,* 8 July 1863.

[22]See vote by counties in *Journal of the Called and Third Regular Annual Session of the House of Representatives, 1863,* 110.

as candidates.'' The ''peace party's'' objectives included ''the encouragement of desertion, the protection of desertees from arrest, [and] resistance to conscription.'' The report said that ''the rank and file of the paroled prisoners of the Vicksburg army . . . contributed largely by their votes to the result of the election,'' and that ''the host of deserters who swarm throughout the country . . . came forth from their lurking places'' to vote.[23]

The right of Alabama soldiers to vote in the election of August 1863 became a controversial one in the months before the election. All of Alabama's wartime governors received letters urging the right of soldiers to the ballot and the judiciary committees of the House and Senate made an extensive study of the subject, but finally decided that the residency requirements of the 1861 constitution could be waived only by a constitutional amendment that could not be secured before August 1863. Under existing law a citizen had to live in the state for the past year and live in the county for the past three months in order to vote.[24] Consequently Alabama soldiers could not take part in the election. The very able Congressman—J. L. M. Curry from the Talladega District—viewed the failure to allow soldiers to vote as a main reason for his defeat. He claimed that the weak, irresolute reconstructionists and peace party advocates were at home to vote while most of the men who shared his convictions about the war were in the army far from the polls.[25] Nevertheless, the Twenty-fifth Alabama Regiment passed resolutions favoring Watts over Shorter in the governor's race. However, the fact that the story of the straw ballot vote taken by the regiment was first printed in a handbill circulated by the ''Friends of Watts for Governor'' suggests that the whole affair may have been a propaganda ploy engineered by the Watts forces.[26]

Watts was elected governor, but the significant aspect for the future of his administration was the broad spectrum of the election. The elected legislature was composed of a large number of obscure Peace party men who would refuse to cooperate in carrying out the war. C. C. Clay, in Montgomery after his own reelection to the Senate, wrote a correspondent that the new legislature was ''composed of a large majority of new men, who

---

[23]W. T. Walthall to G. W. Lay, 6 August 1863, in *OR,* ser. 4, vol. 2, 726-27.

[24]Selma *Reporter,* 24 July 1863.

[25]McMillan, *Alabama Confederate Reader,* 235.

[26]See Handbill by ''Friends of Watts for Governor.''

had never been in office before and of whom I had never heard. None of my old friends in that body could tell of the political sentiments of one in ten of these new men.''[27] Six pacifists and enemies of the Davis administration were sent to Congress. The new legislature would soon replace Yancey and Clay in the Confederate Senate with men of a different stripe. Merely by opposing John Gill Shorter, the longtime ardent secessionist and war prosecutor, Watts, an old Unionist, was—through no fault of his own except his absence from the state and failure to delineate the issues—assumed to be soft on the prosecution of the war. In fact people were so tired of the war that they read into the situation whatever they wanted. Watts did not favor ''reconstruction'' but, as the only alternative to Shorter, he attracted a large following among the Peace party, which had been growing for more than a year.

The election of 1863 was a flagrant breakdown of the democratic process. Seldom, if ever, in the history of democracy have the people been forced to vote so blindly as they did in the gubernatorial election of 1863. This uninformed vote of August 1863 was a direct result of the abandonment of party politics during the war. The ultimate result of the election was to tie the state government in knots. The people had elected a governor, about whom they knew very little, and a legislature, about which they knew a lot, but the governor and the legislature did not share beliefs on any vital issues.[28]

When Watts spoke out after the election, it was too late. ''For myself,'' he wrote, ''I will not forfeit my self-respect by arguing the question of 'reconstruction.' . . . If I had the power, I would build up a *wall of fire* between Yankeedom and the Confederate states, there to burn, for ages, as a monument of the folly, wickedness, and vandalism of the puritanic race!''[29] To squash the belief that he favored ''reconstruction,'' Watts conducted a speaking tour of the northern and middle sections of Alabama after the election. During this tour he convinced even the reconstructionists that he was a ''war man all over.'' After Watts's speech in Talladega,

---

[27]Quoted in Nuermberger, *The Clays of Alabama,* 225; McMillan, *Alabama Confederate Reader,* 235-38.

[28]Montgomery *Weekly Mail,* 23 September 1863; see also McMillan, *Alabama Reader,* 335-37.

[29]Watts to Ira P. Foster, 12 September 1863 in Moore, *Rebellion Record,* 10:238.

a center of reconstruction sentiment, the local editor complained that he filled his speech with the "old state rights, state sovereignty and secession arguments which were not favorably received by our people, a majority of whom never favored secession."[30]

After the election the *Clarke County Journal* advised all Alabamians that if they could keep cool on the issues that defeated Shorter, then "Colonel Watts will make you an able and popular Governor and be deserving of your support for reelection."[31] Those issues were listed as: "impressing your Negroes for defense," "the calling up of every able-bodied man for service," "the salt question and the liquor question," and "peace prices in war time."

The day of celebration accompanying the inaugural of Governor Watts was a gala occasion. The affable and entertaining governor wore a home-spun suit made for the occasion by his mother in Butler County. The band of Watts's old regiment, the Seventeenth Alabama, furnished music for the inauguration at noon and the banquet that night at Watts's home on Adams Street. The Montgomery *Weekly Mail* of 9 December 1863 described the banquet in the evening as "a grand affair attended by the elite of the city. Grave and dignified senators mingled with forms of beauty and loveliness and the strains of sweet music from the band made the scene too agreeable to be forgotten." About the food, the editor wrote, "The delicacies placed before the visitors was [*sic*] so profuse in quantity and so artistically gotten up that none would have imagined hard times to exist in any portion of the Confederacy." The editor implied that the occasion contrasted sharply with what many thousands of Alabamians were undergoing. Wade Keyes, the acting attorney general in Richmond, read the menu in the Montgomery *Advertiser* and wrote the governor, "Oysters in the raw. [I] should like to have been one of the attacking party."[32]

The inaugural dinner proved to be a very short interlude in the tragic drama of the next eighteen months. Writing in 1872, William Garrett said that "never was there a more trying or critical juncture in the experience of any public man" than that suffered by Governor Watts from 1 December 1863, the day of his inauguration, until the fall of Montgomery on 12

---

[30]Quoted in Lynch, "Watts," 20-21.

[31]*Clarke County Journal,* 13 August 1863.

[32]Wade Keys to Gov. Watts, 4 December 1863.

April 1865.[33] Perhaps Watts had come to sense this when he said in his inaugural address that the governorship in peacetime was the "fit reward for a lifetime of public service," but with the increased duties "created by the greatest war of modern times . . . I scarcely know whether thanks are due for the grave responsibilities with which this election clothes me."[34]

As Watts delivered his inaugural, he was well aware of the recent "Bread Riots" in Mobile and the general hunger and suffering in the state but could not afford to give news of the bad situation to the enemy. After his election and some weeks before his inaugural, a number of women in Mobile marched down Dauphine Street breaking open stores and taking bread, bacon, and clothing. They carried banners that proclaimed "Bread or Blood" and "Bread and Peace." However, Watts's inaugural address made it clear that he would favor resistance to the last and would resist any overtures for peace.

Watts's inaugural address also contained a review of events up to 1863, all of which were justified by references to Calhoun's states' rights and state sovereignty theories. According to one account, the address was "so clear and conclusive a defense of the right of the Southern states to secede from the old Federal Union that it was printed by request and a number of copies sent to Europe as an able statement of the question from the Southern standpoint."[35]

Watts was destined to be governor at a time when impressment, the tax-in-kind, and other harsh economic measures became most odious. After Gettysburg and Vicksburg, Confederate money was worth less and less and Confederate credit was impossible to secure, and it was only through impressment and the tax-in-kind that the Confederacy could continue to finance the war. Yet these very measures would turn the people against their own government and contribute to its collapse. The government was in a hopeless quandary. In the short run the Confederacy could finance the war with these harsh measures, but in the long run the same measures would

---

[33]Garrett, *Reminiscences*, 72.

[34]Watts Inaugural Address in *Journal of the Called and Third Regular Annual Session of the House of Representatives, 1863*, 183-89; *Representative Men of the South*, 43.

[35]*Representative Men of the South*, 52. The entire address is printed in this volume, 43-52.

convince many people that they preferred the "Old Union" to the "new despotism."[36]

Although Watts issued a proclamation to the people in an attempt to defend impressment, his inauguration was scarcely over before he protested Confederate impressment policies. On 12 December 1863 he wrote Secretary of War Seddon:

> Complaints from several counties in this state say that Confederate impressment officers are going through the country proposing to impress all the pork over 150 pounds for each member of the family and the work oxen and other stock necessary for farming purposes. These men are creating great disturbance and excitement among the people. Now is the time for killing the pork and the tax-in-kind will soon be paid. If these proceedings are authorized by your authority it is very unfortunate.

He then said that he believed the proceedings were contrary to the law and to orders issued by the adjutant general's office. "The inevitable tendency of all such acts is to harass all the people and to cause many to hide their surplus bacon, pork and beef and to dampen the patriotic ardor of the people." Watts thought the situation all the more questionable since collection of the tax-in-kind on bacon was eminent. That meant that the Confederate government would secure not less than five million pounds in Alabama and perhaps more. He told Seddon that the whole procedure of impressment would "check the disposition to produce and ultimately diminish the supply for public and private use."[37]

In early 1864 J. J. Walker, commissioner of subsistence for Alabama, ordered a census of all the livestock in the state. This immediately aroused the ire and suspicions of the people and the governor's office was flooded with inquiries. The census turned out to be a preparation for the government's requisition of animals before slaughter. After the fall of Vicksburg and the resulting loss of Western beef, the government was hard-pressed to feed the army. It made plans to impress and slaughter its own animals using all parts of the carcass. A lot of unnecessary opposition was caused, Watts said, by not stating the reason for the census in advance. In writing

---

[36]Owsley, *State Rights,* 224-26.

[37]Watts to Seddon, 12 December 1863; Watts to Seddon, 19 January 1864, in *OR,* ser. 4, vol. 3, 37. For Watts's proclamation in defense of impressment, see Selma *Morning Reporter,* 27 May 1864.

to the secretary of war about the matter, he told Seddon: ''The impressment of private property is always odious and ought to be avoided when-
ever possible. It is a better policy for the Government to pay double price
than to make impressments. If we fail to achieve our independence in this
contest,'' he warned, ''the failure will arise from breaking down the spirits
of the people by acts of tyranny from our own officers. The impressment
of property only aggravates the price and creates opposition to the Government and our cause.'' Watts ended the letter to Seddon by saying that
he knew Walker and had full trust in him, despite the fact that he had been
negligent in not letting the people know the purpose of the census in advance. However, Watts added, ''Many of the impressing officers care neither for God nor man.''[38]

The governor received many letters from the people complaining of ir-
regular impressments. The law provided for impressments to be made by
commissary or quartermaster officers but, in their absence, regular army
officers and even privates made impressments—thus abusing the system.
Certificates given in payment by these unauthorized officers were not legally binding and often went unpaid. Many pitiful stories of mistreated
soldiers' families reached the governor. In Tuscaloosa County, far removed from any fighting army, a party of impressment officers took, from
a soldier's family in which there was not a pound of meat, their last milk
cow and dispossessed other families of their cows and horses. The men
sold their plunder only a few miles away, proving that they were posing as
officers. Bogus impressment officers posing as Confederate or state officials took all kinds of property and left behind worthless certificates. Watts
urged the legislature to move against such frauds and in October 1864 the
legislators passed a law that imposed a fine and a two-to-five year prison
sentence for impressment of goods under false pretense.[39]

Nearly all the impressed goods were purchased at much less than fair
market price. The price was fixed by a meeting of all the state commissioners. One of their last meetings was in Montgomery 20 September 1864.
Dissatisfied with the prices at this meeting, the Alabama legislature passed

[38]Watts to Seddon, 19 January 1864, in *OR,* ser. 4, vol. 3, 37.

[39]Cited in Martin, *Desertion of Alabama Troops,* 95; David Hubbard to Gov. Watts,
19 December 1863; H. A. Creeview to Watts, 14 February 1864; J. L. Cunningham and
others to Watts, 18 June 1864; Fleming, *Alabama,* 175-76; *Acts of the Called and Fourth
Regular Annual Session of the General Assembly of Alabama, 1864,* 12.

resolutions asking fair market value for all impressed goods and asserting that certificates for these goods should be made legal tender until such time as the government paid them.[40] When the government abandoned impressment because of resistance from the people in the last months of the war, a half-million dollars in legal certificates throughout the Confederacy remained unpaid. The amount due its citizens was a much greater sum because in the last year of the war the government lacked funds and impressed goods without pretending to pay.[41]

The worst abuse of the impressment system was carried out by the Confederate cavalry, for by its very nature it did not have a supply train. It was able to subsist as it moved by impressing goods. Although generally called foraging, their impressment methods were more honestly referred to as pillage and plunder. E. C. Betts of northern Alabama, later Alabama commissioner of agriculture, wrote to Watts in February 1864 that "the approach of a body of Confederate cavalry fills every neighborhood with dread and any man upon whose premises they camp regards himself as already ruined." Betts thought that the Confederate cavalry was as destructive as the enemy in the Tennessee Valley. He told Watts that "the evils with which the community is afflicted arise from the licentious conduct of the Confederate cavalry who roam the country invading the privacy of families, robbing the farmers of their horses and mules, shooting down or driving off their stock without even consulting the owner—depriving helpless families of their last means of subsistence—committing every species of depredation which usually characterizes the march of a hostile army through a country subjugated by their arms." He said that the command of General Wheeler, on its passage through the region the previous fall, "desolated the wealthiest neighborhoods in North Alabama in twenty-four hours and swept over the whole country from here to Chattanooga like a scourge."[42]

Watts received many complaints that the cavalry, under the command of General Joseph E. Johnston in eastern Tennessee and General Leonidas Polk in northern Mississippi, was raising havoc in northern Alabama. In

---

[40]*Acts of the Called and Fourth Regular Annual Session of the General Assembly of Alabama, 1864,* 12.

[41]Owsley, *State Rights,* 227.

[42]E. C. Betts to Watts, 5 February 1864.

May 1864 William Shepherd of Blount County wrote Watts a bitter letter
about the "Rice gang," composed of cavalry from Johnston's army that
repeatedly sacked Blount County, "stealing, pillaging, and arresting those
who opposed them." He said they had stolen all his horses and mules and
burned his daughter's house.[43] In March 1864 scores of citizens from Talladega County petitioned the governor to stop similar practices in that
county perpetrated by cavalry from Johnston's and Polk's armies. In part
the petition read, "A large number of the force is constantly engaged in
taking the horses and mules belonging to the citizens here, killing stock
hogs, forcibly and unwarrantably impressing corn and fodder, breaking up
tanyards and committing other devious depredations—and to such an extent is this evil carried that there is no security for most of the personal
property of this county." Watts advised the petitioners to organize the
county militia to handle the marauders. Watts and his correspondents knew
that the militia could not take care of the problem, but the governor was
helpless. Watts did argue that if a first-class militia could be organized in
northern Alabama, the cavalry could be withdrawn.[44]

General James H. Clanton wrote Governor Watts that the Confederate
cavalry in northern Alabama was a disgrace to the government, saying:
"Our own cavalry has been a great terror to our own people. . . . Stealing,
robbing, and murdering is quite common." He reported that much of
northern Alabama was so bare that there was no subsistence for his horses,
which were "on the point of starvation."[45] By 1864 the cavalry was usually placed where it could subsist rather than where it could best strike at
the enemy. In December 1864 Watts asked General Taylor to withdraw
five or six companies of cavalry from Walker County as "they are doing
no good there and the eating of the tithe corn is simply depriving a great
many people of bread." Watts suggested to Taylor that if the object of operations was to fatten the horses, he should send these companies to some
rich prairie county in central or southern Alabama, "as the cries of starving people are coming up to me almost everyday" from north Alabama.[46]

------

[43]William Shepherd to Watts, 22 May 1864; Watts to William Shepherd, 4 June 1864.

[44]Petition of Joe H. Johnson et al. to Watts, 22 May 1864; Watts to William Shepherd,
4 June 1864.

[45]James H. Clanton to Watts, 30 March 1864, in *OR,* vol. 32, pt. 3, 718-19.

[46]Watts to Taylor, 9 December 1864.

Watts became exceedingly aroused when the Confederacy tried to impress state property. When a sack of salt that belonged to the state and was intended for the indigent was impressed, he wrote Seddon: "If about half the Confederate quartermasters were dismissed from office and put into the ranks such illegal proceedings would probably cease."[47] When slaves working for the state at the state saltworks were impressed, Watts wrote Jones Withers that they were no more liable to impressment than money in the state treasury. Watts demanded their immediate return, saying that as governor he had only to demand their return to have it done.[48] Actually, General Maury and his chief engineer, Victor von Sheliha, seized state slaves at the state saltworks to send Watts a message. It was becoming much harder to impress slaves. Planters, like everyone else, were reading the news of the battlefield and reacting accordingly. The Mobile commander and his engineer wanted the governor to become more active in enforcing the impressment of slaves. Watts specifically declared that impressment was a Confederate matter provided for under Confederate law and that he did not intend to use the power of his office to impress slaves. Watts's predecessor, Governor Shorter, had used the executive power to impress slaves long before the passage of the Confederate Impressment Act of March 1863.[49]

Another form of impressment was the Confederate government's seizure and total monopoly of the output of mills and factories. Since Alabama was rich in iron ore, the War Department soon had the many small ironworks and few rolling mills under monopolistic contract for the Confederacy. The consequence of the government's policy, Watts wrote Seddon, was that "the planters, even in the best iron regions of the State, cannot get enough iron to make and repair their agricultural implements." He told the secretary of war that without iron, the planting interests, which fed the army and civilian population, would cease to produce. Seddon referred the matter to the Niter and Mining Bureau, which ruled that some cast iron could be spared for agriculture but not much rolling iron because all except

---

[47]Watts to Seddon, 19 January 1864.

[48]Watts to Maury, 12 August 1864; Watts to Jones M. Withers, 3 March 1865.

[49]See Watts to Maury, 16 August 1864, saying that "the State of Alabama declined to make impressments after Congress gave the Confederate authorities the right to make them." Also see Watts to T. I. Cornish, 11 April 1864. Cornish was a Confederate impressing agent asking the governor to use his power in impressing slaves.

two rolling mills in Alabama had been overrun by the enemy. The department encouraged Alabama to start another rolling mill in Selma, but the
effort had to be abandoned because workers at the plant were forced into
the army. Such situations faced the governor at every turn in the last year
of the war. The demand for manpower took skilled labor into the army and
a similar demand for skilled labor in factories tied the whole Confederate
war effort into knots.[50]

A mill in Tuscaloosa had furnished cloth to line the uniforms of University of Alabama cadets for years. Two months before Dr. L. C. Garland, the president of the university, would have made his purchase in 1864,
the mill was seized by Confederate authorities and its whole product taken
by the Confederacy. Garland then wrote Watts that in a search throughout
the Confederacy he had failed to find cloth to line the jackets and panta-
loons of the cadets and that he was now forced to cut the university's bed
sheets for the purpose. Watts begged the War Department to release enough
cloth at the Tuscaloosa mill for the university. The governor's correspondence does not record whether Dr. Garland got the cloth or had to continue
to cut the university's bed sheets.[51]

Fear of impressment became so great that it restricted the normal
movement of goods throughout the state. Food became scarce in some
towns because farmers would not take goods to market lest they be impressed. Less salt was made because so many teams and wagons were impressed at the salt springs. The impressing agents pounced on those who
were the most visible and the easiest to get. Typical of the letters reaching
Watts was one from a salt maker whose mules and wagons had been impressed. "My wagons and mules were impressed at the salt works some
two months ago," he wrote. "I had been engaged making salt about one
year and I gave affadavit [sic] to that effect but they still have my wagons
and mules. Have I any redress? Salt is worth one hundred dollars per sack
and it is not right to prevent the manufacture of it for fear it goes higher."
The record contains no answer to this query; in a similar case the governor
expressed sympathy but said, "The impressments were not made by me

---

[50]Watts to Seddon, 6 January 1864, in *OR*, ser. 4, vol. 3, 3-4; Seddon to Watts, 18
January 1864, ibid., 34.

[51]Watts to Seddon, 1 February 1864. Seddon did not answer Watts's first letter, and in
July Watts sent Garland to Richmond with another letter asking for the cloth. See Watts to
Seddon through President Garland, 29 July 1864.

and I have no right to rescind any orders made by the Confederate authorities."[52]

Watts opposed the tax-in-kind, which bore heavily on the poor and by its very nature was a class tax because it was levied on agriculture alone. When the collector in Tuscaloosa made a demand on the insane asylum for one-tenth of the produce grown by the patients in their garden, the governor became incensed at the impropriety of the act. Dr. J. T. Searcy, superintendent of the asylum, notified Watts and the governor wrote Seddon: "As you know the institution and its produce belong to the state of Alabama. The Confederate government has no right to tax the property of the state."[53]

The tax-in-kind was particularly odious to soldiers' families. Their women and children were not able to make enough corn for their own bread and had to give one-tenth of it to the government. The wives of two soldiers from Bibb County wrote Governor Watts a joint letter asking to be allowed to keep the tithe corn. They argued that this aid to indigent soldiers' wives would save the government and the indigent the expense of transporting the corn. They would need the tithe corn or its equivalent to keep from starving, they declared. Watts wrote the women that all he could do was protest—that the tax was a Confederate one over which "he had no power."[54] The legislature in 1864 passed resolutions petitioning the Confederate Congress to "suspend the tax-in-kind on all produce made with white labor." Watts by proclamation suspended all state taxes in nine enemy-occupied north Alabama counties for 1864.[55]

In the winter of 1863-1864 many people were on the verge of starvation in the hills of northern Alabama and in the poorer counties of southeastern Alabama. On 9 December 1864 Watts wrote General Richard Taylor in connection with getting the food-consuming cavalry out of

---

[52]J. C. Young to Gov. Watts, 8 October 1864; Watts to Messrs. L. N. Nichols and Co., 8 June 1864. In this case, all the slaves of the Bon Secour Salt Company had been impressed to work on the fortifications at Mobile.

[53]Watts to Seddon, 9 December 1864.

[54]Petition from Bibb County to Watts, 24 February 1864 and Watts's answer written on back.

[55]Joint Resolutions of the Legislature in Montgomery *Weekly Advertiser,* 30 December 1864. See proclamation of dismissal of taxes in Montgomery *Daily Mail,* 21 March 1865.

northern Alabama since "the cries of starving people are coming up to me almost every day from that section." Watts was aware that the main problem in feeding all Alabamians was one of transportation. To save themselves and their starving children, women had to walk miles with sacks on their backs to secure corn in the Black Belt and other rich agricultural areas.

These conditions existed despite the fact that over time the legislature had appropriated $8 million to buy corn for indigent soldiers' families since Watts became governor. On 12 December 1863 the legislature appropriated $3 million to be distributed in three equal payments of $1 million to be made in January, May, and October 1864. During the called session of September 1864, the legislature provided for another $2 million for distribution; the regular session in November provided another $3 million. Although the regular session did increase taxes by fifty percent and the state continued to sell its somewhat "shaky bonds," most of the funds to finance these large appropriations were met by simply printing more state treasury notes, which in turn continued to reduce their buying power. The latter acts provided that, if possible, the probate judges and commissioners in all counties were to buy supplies for distribution and to distribute money only if supplies were not available.[56] Watts urged the county officials to send agents to the rich agricultural areas of central and southern Alabama to get corn. Ex-Governor Moore was still offering his good offices and experience in purchasing grain in the rich areas for northern Alabama probate judges. The quartermaster's office wrote Governor Watts in March 1864 that Moore had purchased "some one hundred and odd thousand bushels of corn, most of it to be delivered after the planting season was over, but a problem had arisen because most of the planters would not take anything but the new issue of currency in payment."[57]

There was little difficulty in finding corn in central and southern Alabama; the problem was in getting it transported and distributed to the needy areas. Although Watts had spent much time denouncing impressments, he

---

[56]*Acts of the Called and Third Regular Annual Session of the General Assembly of Alabama, 1863*, 82; ibid., 5-7, 58-61; Fleming, *Alabama*, 168; Howard, "Alabama State Currency," 78-82.

[57]Watts to Captain M. Davenport, 21 April 1864; Quartermaster's Office to Watts, 18 March 1864. By law of 17 February 1864, the Confederate Congress repudiated one-third of the value of its old currency by exchanging all its treasury notes above five dollars for new paper worth one-third less.

declared that "if wagons cannot be got otherwise, they must be impressed to haul corn for the poor." The legislature had not made a direct appropriation for hauling supplies for the indigent families, but Watts directed that state funds be so used.[58] The legislature and the governor tried to solve the transportation problem by authorizing Watts to buy corn near railroads and rivers. This corn was to be traded to the Confederacy for tithe corn in isolated areas so that there would be no hauling involved.[59]

The same areas where people faced starvation were those where the population had to contend with lawless bands variously made up of deserters—Tories or Unionists—disaffected Confederates, bushwhackers, and just plain criminals. In many counties it was a real civil war in which brothers or relatives fought on opposite sides. Numerous letters in Watts's executive files tell of the depredations of these lawless bands, but there was little Watts could do since order was generally kept in these situations by a well-organized militia and the governor's hands were tied in regard to the militia by legislative restrictions. County militia, confined to their county of residence, were available but were so infiltrated by the lawless bands that they were useless.

Letters to the governor indicate that these bands of lawless men committed almost every crime—from stealing to murder. They went from house to house demanding provisions, clothing, guns, and ammunition. They shot or seized livestock; they robbed travelers and fell upon the helpless everywhere. They burned the property of secessionists—their houses, corncribs, and mills. Special delight was taken in torturing the wealthy. Courthouses were burned to destroy records that might incriminate these marauders. They forced many whole families to flee their homes and become refugees in central and southwest Alabama. Sheriffs and probate judges were seized because they were symbols of the law. They murdered them sometimes and always subjected them to manhandling and other indignities. In some areas judges refused to hold court without sufficient military protection. In January 1865 Judge John Cochran, who succeeded Shorter as judge of the Eighth Judicial District in southeast Alabama, de-

---

[58]Watts to Captain M. Davenport, 21 April 1864; Watts to Colonel I. S. Sheffield, 25 April 1864.

[59]*Acts of the Called and Fourth Regular Annual Session of the General Assembly of Alabama, 1864,* 47.

clared that he had not held court in Coffee and Dale counties for the last two years and would hold no court in these counties "unless protected by the military." A petition from Henry County to Governor Watts of 23 March 1864 is typical:

> These bands now number in both counties [Henry and Dale] upwards of 300 men and are generally well armed and stand in bold defiance of all law and authority and are fast becoming a terror to all peaceable men and women. They have murdered, within the last twelve months, four good and loyal citizens; they have stripped several plantations of mules and horses and burnt to the ground several cribs of corn. They have plundered a great many houses and stolen from them guns, ammunition, clothing, provisions and other property and have appropriated the same to their own use and they constantly lay in ambush on our public roads with the avowed intentions of assassinating all who may endeavor in the execution of the law to thwart their plans or arrest them.[60]

The most spectacular tragedy in all this lawlessness—in which Confederates suffered the most—was the killing of T. P. Curtis, the probate judge of Winston County, for his Union sympathies. This murder was perpetrated by a band of men who still had some connections with the Confederate cavalry. The charge was that he had given state supplies for indigent families to families of men who had joined the Union army. In demanding that punishment be meted out to the killers, Governor Watts wrote Lieutenant Colonel Lockhart that "no punishment is too great for such men." As the story unfolded, the bad character of the killers became more apparent. After seizing the judge, they forced his wife to get them the keys to the jail, where salt for the indigent was kept. They took the judge to a secluded spot in the direction of Jasper and executed him; his body could not be found for days. They sold the salt and divided the money among themselves. Watts declared that "such conduct will do more injury to our cause than a Yankee Raid."[61]

----

[60]Josiah Jones to Governor Watts, 20 March 1865; Nancy M. Twillery to Watts, 9 November 1864; J. M. Carmichael to Watts, 17 October 1864; C. D. Losseter and Wilie Duffee to Watts, 27 February 1865; Petition from Henry County to Watts, 23 March 1864; James N. Arrington, Solicitor for the Eighth District, to Jones M. Withers, 30 January 1865, in *OR*, ser. 4, vol. 3, 1043.

[61]Watts to Lieut. Col. Lockhart, 6 February 1864.

Salt continued to be a scarce item and a very speculative commodity during the Watts administration. The making and distribution of salt was reorganized by Watts under an act of the August 1863 legislature. Duff C. Green, the quartermaster general of the state, was given tighter controls over the collection and distribution of salt. His office was moved from Mobile, where it had been under Moore and Shorter, to Montgomery, where he could be close to the governor.[62] During Watts's first months in office, there were widespread rumors of fraud among some northern Alabama salt agents. R. B. Kyle, salt agent at Gadsden, wrote the governor that salt in state sacks was being used by speculators in that area. Watts moved rapidly to stop speculation and fraud in the system. He issued an order that any sack of salt marked with the Alabama insignia was prima facie evidence and that it belonged to the state and should be seized. B. M. Woolsey, lawyer and planter of Selma, was appointed salt commissioner for the state, subject to Green's supervision, to replace Abner McGehee, who had notified the governor he wished to resign.[63]

The state manufacture of salt from the salt springs in Clarke and nearby counties continued to flourish. When some friction developed between Alabama and Mississippi salt makers, Watts wrote Governor Charles Clark of Mississippi that he was welcome to make salt in the same area as long as Mississippi contractors did not interfere with the state reservations. The Alabama Salt Springs supplied most of the salt for Alabama, Mississippi, and west Georgia throughout the war.[64]

The salt supply from Saltville, Virginia, dried up early in the Watts administration. First, the Saltville makers wanted to price their salt in terms of gold, which Watts refused. Second, transportation by railroad became impossible as Federal armies penetrated deeper into the South. To compensate for the loss of Virginia salt, Watts contracted for the making of salt from sea water along the coast of Alabama and Florida and especially at West Bay, Florida. Salt makers along the coast became subject to repeated raids from Federal gunboats along with raids from deserters and ruffians in the Wiregrass country. Iron was almost impossible to secure and each

[62]Watts to Duff C. Green, 8 January 1864.

[63]Watts to R. B. Kyle, 5 December 1863; Watts to B. M. Woolsey, 31 December 1863; Watts to Alexander Snodgrass, 5 December 1863.

[64]Watts to Gov. Charles Clark of Mississippi, 28 May 1864.

raid destroyed, at least partially, the salt kettles and other equipment.[65] The law did not allow Watts to send the militia out of the state, so he organized two volunteer companies to protect the salt makers against these raids. One of these companies, an artillery unit, was promised guns by General Maury, but the enemy attack on Mobile Bay in August 1864 forced Watts to send the troops to Mobile and suspend his request for the guns.[66] These manufactures then had to be abandoned as the Federal fleet was concentrated between Pensacola and Mobile for the final attack on Mobile. In the last months of the war, unless one was lucky enough to get salt from Clarke County, it could not be secured at all and brought astronomical prices on the open market.

As manpower for the army became more scarce in the last years of the war, the enrolling officers were always after the salt makers. They were easier to find than the deserters and eligible conscripts hiding in the woods, caves, coves, and swamps. In 1864 a company making salt in the Mobile Bay area had all of its Negroes impressed to work on the fortifications of Mobile. As mentioned earlier, individual planters were afraid to send their Negroes and teams to the salt springs or to any public place for fear they would be impressed. As the enrolling and impressment officers continued to harass salt makers and other state interests, Watts wrote Secretary of War Seddon in January 1865: "Your enrolling officers are very diligent in finding out how they can annoy the state while they overlook many who ought to be in the service."[67]

One of the charges made by the "Friends of Watts" against Shorter in the 1863 campaign was that he had neglected the making of cards that made possible the manufacture of clothing by household methods. Watts made an extra effort to secure cards at home and abroad. Shorter entered a contract subsidizing John Kemp of Selma in the manufacture of cards, but Kemp was not very successful in turning out a workable product. Watts cancelled the contract. He then authorized the Reverend J. C. Davis of Montgomery to make cards for the state with a machine he had invented

---

[65]Watts to Messrs. McLung and Jaques, 20 April 1864. Bessie Martin has a discussion of these attacks in her *Desertion of Alabama Troops,* 195.

[66]Watts to Jones M. Withers, 9 August 1864; Watts to Dabney H. Maury, 16 June 1864.

[67]Watts to Secretary of War Seddon, 3 January 1865.

that allegedly would turn out seventy-five pairs a day. The greatest deterrent to home manufacture of cards was the lack of wire.[68]

Watts also tried to bring cards through the blockade. On 21 April 1864 he wrote a correspondent that he had "run the blockade with about two thousand pairs of cards" and intended to bring in twenty thousand more. Watts's letters do not indicate how many more he got through, but it was probably very few since Mobile Bay was captured in August. The letters do indicate that he was able to get some through to the port of Wilmington, North Carolina, for he wrote Seddon asking for a permit to ship the cards by rail to Alabama. He told the secretary that they were military goods because without them Alabama soldiers and their families could not be clothed.[69] On another occasion he asked the War Department for a permit to trade through the lines on the Mississippi or Red rivers 300 boxes of tobacco for "Yankee cards." The letters do not indicate whether he got permission to trade through the lines, but he told the legislature in November 1864 that although he had made contracts abroad for more than thirty thousand cards he had received cards from only one of the contractors, "due to the increasing closeness of the blockade."[70] Although Watts's efforts did make more cards available, he could not possibly supply the demand.

In the summer of 1864 Governor Watts ordered all foreigners to enroll for military service or leave the state. The feeling against aliens in the Confederacy had been smoldering for a long time. Many felt that the foreigners did not have to risk their lives and were able to reap the profits of a wartime economy. Any move against them was postponed for a time by the hope of foreign aid, but late in the war all hope for such aid was gone. In quick succession the governors of Georgia, Alabama, and Florida ordered foreigners to enroll for conscription or leave their states. As attorney general, Watts had ruled that foreigners who showed no signs of changing their

---

[68]Watts to John Kemp, 4 January 1864. See report of General Joel Riggs, whom Watts assigned to close out contract with Kemp, in Watts Papers, ADAH. Kemp had made and delivered to the state 516 pairs of cards. Watts's operations with Davis are set forth in a letter to Withers, 28 October 1864, in which he asks that the operators of the card machines not be conscripted.

[69]Watts to Col. Enoch Aldridge, 21 April 1864; Watts to Sec. of War Seddon, 25 April 1864.

[70]Watts to Sec. Seddon, 30 December 1863; Governor's Message to the Legislature, November 1864, in Memphis *Daily Appeal,* 17 November 1864.

domicile were liable to conscription. A concerned President Davis said that although he did not think any of the governors in their proclamations intended to force skilled foreign labor out of the Confederacy, he thought the broad language of their proclamations would force all foreigners to comply. Therefore the president dispatched a circular to Watts and five other Confederate governors, all of whom had presumably issued proclamations, asking them to modify their proclamations or let it be known that foreign laborers holding essential jobs in the Confederacy would not be conscripted. Perhaps the key line in the president's circular said, "Those aliens even who are laboring elsewhere than in the service of the Government are efficiently aiding our cause by services of great value in furnishing to our people many necessary articles, such as shoes, clothing, machinery, agricultural implements, and the like, which it is now so difficult to obtain from abroad."[71]

Watts had once been a member of the American, or Know-Nothing, party and this apparently made members of minority groups sensitive to his words and actions. In issuing a call to the people of Alabama for a day of consecration and prayer, he headed his proclamation "To all the Christian people of Alabama." Rabbi Gutheim of the Montgomery synagogue took offense and charged the governor with excluding the Jews although they had done much for the Confederate cause. Watts tried to explain to him that the Jews were included—and that what he meant was all people of religious faiths. The rabbi was still sorely offended and there was an exchange of many letters, some of which were published in the newspapers of the period.[72]

The need to raise troops for the defense of the state became increasingly urgent. Watts's administration had scarcely begun before all of Alabama's borders became exposed to military invasion. The enemy remained in northern Alabama and was intensifying the war there. After the fall of Vicksburg in the summer of 1863, most of Mississippi came under enemy control; and all of Alabama was liable to invasion from the west, the grand prizes being Mobile—the largest city in the state—and Selma. After the

---

[71]For French consular protests against action of Confederate governors, see *OR*, ser. 3, vol. 4, 780-81; Ella Lonn, *Foreigners in the Confederacy* (Chapel Hill, 1940) 387-88, 394-98; Davis's circular letter to Watts and other governors, in *OR*, ser. 4, vol.3, 670-71.

[72]For letters and newspaper clippings about the Rabbi and Watts, see Watts Collection, Manuscript Room, ADAH.

fall of Atlanta and Sherman's march to the sea late in 1864, eastern Alabama was also vulnerable. The Confederate army was near depletion and the time had come when only the militia was left to defend the state. A strong militia could not be organized unless the Militia Act of August 1863 could be changed. The act created an awkward two-class militia. Class-one was the county reserves (estimated by Watts at 30,000 men), who could not be ordered out of their county of residence. Class-two was the state reserves (estimated at fewer than 5,000 men when created), whom the governor could use anywhere within the state but could not send out of the state. The state reserves were seriously weakened after December 1863 because Congress abolished the substitute system and extended the age limit for conscripts.[73]

Watts's only recourse, other than getting the legislature to change the law, was to appeal to the male population to form volunteer companies or to get the county reserves to agree to serve in the state reserves. He issued appeals on 6 and 17 February 1864 after Mobile was threatened by Federal troops in Mississippi. He again made appeals on 22 July and 4 August during the period of Lovell H. Rousseau's raid from north Alabama against the Montgomery and West Point Railroad in east-central Alabama. Rousseau reached the road easily and destroyed it between Tuskegee and Opelika. This effectively cut off supplies to besieged Atlanta and convinced Watts of the the need for a strengthened militia. He pleaded with the county reserves to rally with the state reserves at Opelika, Montgomery, Selma, and Mobile where they would be armed and organized. He later told the legislature that "the response was negligible."[74]

Perhaps because he knew the composition of the legislature, Watts seemed to hesitate to call it into special session. Governor Shorter had failed to get a strong militia organized before the same legislators. The grim mil-

---

[73]For an extended discussion of how the Militia Act had been weakened, see Watts's message to the legislature in "Manuscript Journal of the called session of the House of Representatives, Sept.-Oct., 1864." There is no printed journal of the legislature of Alabama in its two sessions in 1864, and only the Called Session and the Regular Session of the House Journal is available in manuscript. Therefore, I had to search the newspapers diligently in researching these two sessions.

[74]Proclamations in the Mobile *Advertiser and Register,* 16 February 1864; Gainesville *Independent,* 27 February, 4, 11 August 1864. Most of the proclamations are also filed with the governor's letters. Watts wrote Maury on 16 August 1864 that he would call the legislature into session if he had any hope that it would act. See *OR,* vol. 39, pt. 2, 780.

itary situation, the negative response from the county reserves, and pressure from Confederate leaders made Watts aware that it must be done. The most urgent calls for state troops were coming from Jefferson Davis; Daniel H. Maury, commander at Mobile; and Richard Taylor, commander of the military district of Alabama, Mississippi, and East Louisiana—all indicating that if Mobile was to be reinforced, it would have to be by Alabama and Mississippi state troops. By late August Maury was growing impatient with Governor Watts. He wrote President Davis, "If Mississippi gives 8,000 militia Alabama owes 10,000. Will Your Excellency induce her Governor to convene Legislature and force out all able to fight?"[75] A decision could not be delayed because Farragut's fleet was in Mobile Bay, and both forts at the mouth of the bay had been captured by the enemy. Taylor, who had just moved his headquarters from Meridian to Selma, made a trip to Montgomery in early September 1864 to talk to Watts about the military situation and the need for the Alabama militia. Taylor then wrote Secretary of War Seddon that Watts had promised him sufficient militia to defend Mobile once the special session had reorganized the militia. When Maury wrote President Davis to hasten the resolution of the matter, Davis replied: "It will take time to convene the legislature and I think the Governor already possesses full power on the subject of the militia." Apparently Davis did not know that the Alabama legislature had given the governor only limited control of the militia.[76]

As Watts prepared to call the legislature into special session on the militia issue, he revealed his innermost thoughts to General Maury, who was facing the fatal hour in the defense of Mobile. He wrote: "In the hurry and turmoil of your business I sympathize with you. I have my own cares which I endeavor to bear with becoming patience. I have not been pleased with the disposition of our people to respond to my orders and appeals; so many try to hatch up some excuse for not obeying the orders." Watts especially complained that "the men who have given bonds as agriculturists—many

---

[75]Maury to Davis, 31 August 1864, in *OR*, vol. 52, pt. 2, 727; Davis to D. H. Maury, 2 September 1864, ibid., vol. 39, pt. 2, 812; Seddon to Watts, 2 September 1864, ibid., Maury to Watts, 28 August 1864, ibid., 802.

[76]Richard Taylor to James A. Seddon, 25 September 1864, ibid., 872-73; Davis to Maury, 2 September 1864. Taylor gives an extended account of his visit to Montgomery in his book *Destruction and Reconstruction,* Richard B. Harwell, ed. (New York, 1955) 248-50.

of them—have used all sorts of shifts to avoid militia duty. The militia laws as they now stand are almost worthless.''[77]

The fall of Atlanta on 2 September 1864 triggered Watts's call for a special session of the legislature to reorganize Alabama's militia. The legislature met on 26 September and in his message the governor pointed out that the second-class militia, since it was created in August 1863, had been reduced to almost nothing by the laws of Congress. ''On the 5th day of January 1864, Congress,'' he said, ''had taken a large body of men from the state militia by abolishing the substitute system. On 17 February 1864 Congress further reduced the militia by extending the Conscription law to include seventeen-year olds and men between the ages of forty-five and fifty.'' He called the session to appeal to the legislature to place all able-bodied men from sixteen to fifty-five who were not in the Confederate army into one state militia, thus abolishing restrictions on the governor's use of them. Only state civil and military officers were to be exempt. As commander in chief, he wanted the right to use the militia to defend any part of the state and if he saw fit, to send them into an adjoining Confederate state. He declared, ''The fearful struggle now going on in Georgia is no idle spectacle to Alabama.'' He thought ''the fate of Alabama may be even now being decided in Georgia.''

The August 1863 militia law failed to organize the first-class militia in those counties contained in the three northern Alabama congressional districts. These were enemy-occupied counties and those to the south were disorganized by frequent enemy recruiting and raiding parties. Watts now asked that the militia in these counties be encompassed in the reorganization.[78]

As to the first-class militia being restricted to their county of residence, Governor Watts showed the absurdity of such by depicting a dramatic, hypothetical situation in which a great battle raged in Montgomery while the Autauga County militia watched from the other bank of the Alabama River; yet, he had no power to order them across the river to participate. He reminded them that Alabama's military situation became more critical by the

---

[77]Watts to Maury, 16 August 1964, in *OR,* vol. 39, pt. 2, 780.

[78]Watts's address to called session of the Legislature in ''Manuscript Journal of the House of Representatives, 1864,'' 150-54, also printed in Montgomery *Daily Mail,* 27 September 1864.

day. "The successful advance of the enemy into our sister state of Georgia and the fall of Atlanta have exposed to attack and invasion the northeastern and eastern portions of Alabama," he declared. The fall of Mobile Bay, the capture of Forts Gaines and Morgan, and the threatened attack on Mobile all "call loudly for additional legislation and for prompt action in strengthening the militia," he said. Referring to the large number of "Tories, deserters, stragglers and traitors," in northern Alabama, he argued that he needed a strong and responsible militia to keep them under control. Rousseau's recent raid, he said, had pinpointed Alabama's weakness to raids from the northern part of the state.[79]

The session lasted only twelve days and adjourned *sine die*. A bill passed by the Senate placed every able-bodied white man between the ages of seventeen and fifty-five, and not in the Confederate army, in the militia and gave the governor unrestricted command of them within the state. The House of Representatives refused to go along, opposing the extension of the age limit from fifty to fifty-five and the lifting of restrictions tying the first-class militia to the county of residence. The debate in the House indicated that a majority of that body were of the opinion that Congress had already placed in the army "all the men out of which it would be just and wise to form a militia." Lewis Parsons, the leader of the opposition in the House, argued that the state did not need an organized militia because the Confederate government had full power in the premises—that is, it had the power to recruit all able-bodied men of every age. In the House debate, much emphasis was placed on the need to keep the militia as close to home as possible in order to produce food for the army and civilian population.[80] On 20 September 1864, the editor of the Troy *Southern Advertiser* recorded the arguments regarding the militia as follows: "Our authorities are infatuated on the subject of sending men to the army"; "an organized militia will be absorbed by the Confederate army"; and "without a home producing force everything will be lost." Another position argued that Watts was removed from reality by his high position and that if he knew of the suffering and hardships of the people, he would not ask for further sacrifices.

---

[79]Ibid.

[80]Montgomery *Daily Mail,* 28 September 1864.

Some critics of Watts thought the governor was focusing on the wrong issue. Instead of placing old men and young boys in the militia where they would "become food for hospitals," it would be better to force two-thirds of the men who were absent without leave back into the army. The governor and the legislature acknowledged this viewpoint when they appealed to stragglers and deserters to return to the army while the debate raged over the militia bill. The legislature even issued joint resolutions asking the men to return so that the governor was not forced to fill their places with old men and boys. "Will you force the sires and striplings of the land to fight your battles?" they asked.[81]

Another point of view was expounded by the editor of the Memphis *Daily Appeal*. On 30 September 1864 the editor said that if the old men and boys would not fight to save their hearthstones, property, liberty, and country on a voluntary basis, they would not fight if Watts ordered them into the field.

When a committee of the legislature met with the governor to tell him they were adjourning without reorganizing the militia, he sent a message to the legislature saying that "your failure to act may result in the most calamitous consequences to the state. It is not within my power under the present laws to have it properly defended. It was within your power, but you refused." A little more than a month later, the governor carried the issue over into the regular session of the legislature that met in mid-November. The Senate attempted to mollify the House by restricting the governor to calling up the militia for forty days at a time, but again the issue could not be resolved. The failure by the legislature to act meant that Alabama—and hence the Confederacy—would be denied an effective Alabama militia in the last crucial months of the war. It left a large body of men in the state under no governmental control.[82]

----

[81]Mobile *Tribune*, copied in Montgomery *Daily Advertiser*, 3 October 1864; Watts's proclamation pleading with deserters to return in "Governor's Letter Book," 30 September 1864, ADAH; Joint resolutions of the legislature pleading with deserters to return in *Acts of Alabama for 1864*, 44-48, also printed in Gainesville *Independent*, 18 November 1864.

[82]Governor's letter to Called Session, 7 October 1864; Governor's Message to Regular Session of the legislature, November-December 1864, in Memphis *Daily Appeal*, 17 November 1864. The Troy *Southern Advertiser*, 9 December 1864, has an account of the attempt to compromise.

In September, while the special session was in progress, President Davis appeared in Montgomery on one of his swings through the Confederacy. Apparently the two events coincided by mere chance, but he was invited to address the legislature on the state of the Confederacy. He learned personally from Governor Watts and his own observation of the bad state of affairs in Alabama. Although the president exhorted the legislature to follow the "wise policies and great leadership" of Governor Watts, considering President Davis's lack of popularity in the state by this time, and the Confederate government's reputation for absorbing the militia, the presence of Davis probably hurt Watts's chance of getting a reorganized militia.[83] Certainly his presence embarrassed those who had introduced bills for a negotiated peace. However, the president went away convinced that the measure most needed was a "general militia law" granting Confederate authorities the power "to provide for organizing, arming, and disciplining the militia." As proof he cited the case of Alabama, where "I have been informed by the Governor . . . that the law does not permit him to call the militia from one county for service in another, so that a single brigade of the enemy could traverse the State and devastate each county in turn" while the governor looked on helplessly.[84]

Walter L. Fleming declared that "the stupid conduct of the legislature during the last two years of the war in failing to provide for the defense of the state cannot be too strongly condemned. The final result would have been the same but a strong force of militia would have enabled Governor Watts to execute the laws in all parts of the state, and to protect the families of loyal citizens from outrage by Tories and deserters." He concluded that "jealousy of Confederate authority" was the main reason why the Alabama legislature confined the bulk of the militia to the county of residence—thus making the militia worthless for any organized or concerted aid to the state or the Confederacy. This jealousy of the Confederacy is borne out by the fact that the special session that refused to reorganize the militia also passed a law against any Confederate officer commanding any

---

[83]Davis reached Montgomery on the evening of 28 September and addressed the legislature about noon the next day. See Montgomery *Daily Mail,* 20 September 1864; Memphis *Daily Appeal,* 30 September 1864. Taylor has an interesting account of the president's visit to Montgomery in *Destruction and Reconstruction,* 250-52.

[84]Message of President Davis to the Confederate Congress, 13 March 1865, in *OR,* ser. 4, vol. 3, 1133.

of the Alabama Militia. The opposition to the reorganization of the militia pointed out that the Confederacy did absorb most of Alabama's second-class militia when it passed the Conscription Act of February 1864.[85]

The reorganization of the militia was not the only turbulent issue before the called session of September 1864. The center of controversy was again in the House of Representatives. A peace faction led by Lewis Parsons (soon to be appointed provisional governor) introduced resolutions in favor of opening negotiations for peace. The resolutions declared that the Confederacy should make peace on the basis of the Democratic Chicago platform of 1864 and could negotiate on the basis of equality since it had consistently won on the Virginia front while the Union had won in the West. In anticipation of such a move, Governor Watts's address to the opening session denounced the reconstructionists who wished to rejoin a union with those "who have murdered our sons, outraged our women and destroyed our property." He added that those seeking a negotiated peace "would stamp with infamy alike the names of our gallant dead and living heroes of the war."[86]

The resolutions for a negotiated peace were tabled by the opposition when they were introduced. When its proponents tried to take them from the table and refer them to a special committee, the move was rejected. After some debate, the resolutions were voted on and defeated by a vote of forty-five to thirty-two. The Montgomery *Advertiser* declared that those in the House seeking peace were "insignificant," but more than a third of the House voted for the opening of peace negotiations. On the other hand, the Montgomery *Post* declared that the resolutions would have passed the House except for the "inopportune presence of Jefferson Davis in Montgomery" at the time of the vote. Watts explained in an address to the regular session that opened in mid-November 1864 why he felt there could not be a negotiated peace. This may have forestalled peace resolutions in that session.[87]

---

[85]Fleming, *Alabama,* 90-92; *Acts of the Called and Fourth Regular Annual Session of the General Assembly of Alabama, 1864,* 7-9; Martin, *Desertion,* 210.

[86]See "Proposed Joint Resolutions for Peace" in Montgomery *Daily Mail,* 4 October 1864; Governor's Message in "Manuscript Journal of the House, 1864," 151-53.

[87]Gainesville *Independent,* 8 October 1864; "Manuscript Journal of the Special Session, 1864 of the House of Representatives of the State of Alabama," 162, 181; Montgomery Daily *Advertiser,* 3 October 1864; Montgomery *Daily Post,* 30 June 1865; Governor's Message to Regular Session in Memphis *Daily Appeal,* 17 November 1864.

As the war continued manpower in the Confederacy became nearly as scarce as arms had been in 1861. A conflict between the Confederate and state governments for the remaining men was inevitable. The Conscription Act of 17 February 1864 created the Confederate state reserves, which was composed of males between the ages seventeen and eighteen and from forty-five to fifty, leaving all men from eighteen to forty-five in the regular army. The State Militia Act of August 1863 placed many of the men claimed for the Confederate state reserves in the second-class militia under Watts's command. This was bound to create a clash between Confederate and state authorities. The Confederacy soon put its so-called state reserves under the command of a regular army officer, Jones M. Withers, thus taking them from Watts's control. Another complicating factor was the absence of adequate state manpower as Watts defined it. Watts, like Shorter before him, had created volunteer companies who were under the command of the governor and who were composed of the same men that the Confederacy was now claiming. An ensuing problem occurred in many of the Confederate states. Each year the Confederate congress changed its conscription laws to encompass more of the existing manpower. In earlier years those age groups with members who were not subject to Confederate control were formed into companies by the states under the control of their governors. As the war was ending and local defense problems and disorders were increasing, the governors were reluctant to relinquish the remaining manpower under their control. In addition, the men in these old organizations always resisted the dissolution of their units.[88]

When the enrolling officers attempted to disband the governor's volunteer companies—his troops of last resort—and send the men to conscript camps of instruction, an angry Watts sharply criticized the entire policy of conscription. He said that the methods of the conscription officers were very harmful. He felt that it was sheer nonsense to take productive men from the farms and place them in instruction camps where they would remain inactive and without arms. He further reasoned that in volunteer organizations they could drill periodically and work their farms the rest of the time. He called the Confederate government's policy "the most

---

[88]Albert B. Moore, *Conscription and Conflict in the Confederacy* (Chicago, 1924) 242-43, 308; Coulter, *The Confederate States of America,* 314-15; Walter L. Fleming, "Conscription and Exemption in Alabama during the Civil War," *Gulf States Historical Magazine* 2 (1903-1904): 310-25.

egregious folly'' and wrote, as he liked to do, directly to the president saying that he regarded such action as ''a great calamity—one doing the grossest injustice to the officers and young men.'' Many of them, he told Davis, ''are sons of the most influential citizens of the state.'' If he had to give them up, he thought faith should be kept with the young men by allowing them to be received as organized. They had elected their own officers and had been promised that their units would remain intact. Moreover, he wrote Secretary of War Seddon, the Confederate Constitution guarantees the states ''the right of troops in time of war.''[89]

As the impasse continued, Watts wrote Seddon: ''I have resisted, by remonstrance, the action of the enrolling officers and I may feel myself justified in going farther unless some stop is put to the matter by you.'' When Seddon did not answer, Watts sent a telegraphic ultimatum: ''Unless you order the commandant of conscripts to stop interfering with such companies, there will be a conflict between the Confederate general and State authorities.'' This brought a letter virtually conceding Watts's position. It was the president's opinion, Seddon wrote, that in this case ''it would seem proper to receive the companies as organized either in the reserve or active force.'' Thus Watts won at least part of his demands. The companies would not be broken up and the officers would keep their positions.[90]

Other cases continued to arise under the Confederate State Reserve Act of February 1864. Watts's contention was that the Confederacy had no right to conscript men already in the state service at the time the law was passed until such time as the state discharged them. He issued orders to his units to refuse to release any of the state's men to the enrolling officers. If a Confederate enrolling officer tried to take men from the state units, Watts said he would be arrested. The legislature backed the governor in this opposition to the Confederacy. It imposed a fine of from $1,000 to $6,000 and imprisonment for six months to two years upon conscript officers who forced members of the state's volunteer organizations into Confederate service and it repealed its former law, passed under Shorter, that made of-

---

[89]Watts to Davis, 27 April 1864, in *OR*, ser. 4, vol. 3, 322-23; Watts to Seddon, 31 May 1864, ibid., 463.

[90]Watts to Seddon, 3 June 1864, ibid., 466; Seddon to Watts, ibid., 472.

ficers in the state militia liable to conscription.[91] As the struggle continued
some accommodation was worked out. The Confederate state reserves were
able to take men who were not in the regular army and who were between
the ages of seventeen and fifty while the state got the sixteen-year olds and
men from fifty to sixty. Several months before the war ended, the Alabama
Supreme Court ruled against Governor Watts in the case. It declared that
a soldier's membership in a state organization before the Conscription Act
of February 1864 did not exempt him from surrender when the Confederacy wished to enroll him.[92]

Watts came into office during the second wave of the desertion of Alabama troops from the army following Gettysburg and Vicksburg. Unfortunately for him, he was still in office when the third and final wave of
desertion began after the fall of Atlanta, bringing a rapid deterioration of
life on the home front. The economy disintegrated under the weight of inflation after the totally effective Union blockade that came with the fall of
the port of Mobile. After frequent clashes with Colonel H. C. Lockhart,
in charge of conscription in Alabama, and with Jones M. Withers, commander of the Confederate state reserves, Watts wrote directly to President
Davis asking to be given control of conscription in Alabama. The president submitted Watts's request through Seddon to Colonel John S. Preston, superintendent of the Bureau of Conscription, who advised Davis that
Watts's plan would not work. "I still believe that the very worst agency
to have control of conscription, except that of generals commanding is the
local civil or military authorities," he said. Preston told Davis, "If the State
authorities or generals commanding would actively and cordially co-op-
erate with the conscript authorities instead of endeavoring to control or op-
pose them good might result. During my six months in this Bureau there
has never been one man sent to the field by State authority."[93] In the end
Watts's request was denied. Watts had made his bid and lost. Bypassing
the secretary of war and other officials, Watts presented his ideas and ap-

---

[91]Watts to Col. H. C. Lockhart, 25 January 1865; Acts of 12, 13 December 1864; Fleming, *Alabama*, 98.

[92]Thomas A. Smith, "Mobilization of the Army in Alabama, 1859-1865" (Master's
thesis, Auburn University, 1953) 56; *Alabama Reports* (Montgomery, 1868) 609-10.

[93]Martin, *Desertion*, 26; John S. Preston to Seddon, 18 March 1864, in *OR*, ser. 4, vol.
3, 224-25; Moore, *Conscription and Conflict*, 313.

peals to the president on this and other occasions. He apparently felt that he could write directly to the president because of his status as a former cabinet member.

As with other Confederate manpower controversies, Watts insisted that cadets at the University of Alabama could not be conscripted. Formerly the War Department had given tacit approval to Governor Shorter's claim that cadets at the university were a part of the state and as such could not be conscripted. However, as the war ended the Confederate government was scraping bottom for the manpower to keep an army in the field. The enrolling officers began harassing the cadets. Working with the governor in 1863, the Board of Trustees of the university ordered that in the future no man eighteen or older be allowed to enroll unless exempt from military service. However, Watts insisted that those already in the corps on reaching the age of eighteen were not liable to conscription because they were already in a valid war unit under the control of the governor. Indeed, they were used to train recruits all over the state for the Confederacy and were generally at the call of the governor for any purpose, including the support of Confederate forces. In 1864 trouble ensued when enrolling officers tried to take cadets as they turned eighteen. More serious trouble occurred when enrolling officers tried to take four cadets who had previously been exempted through substitutes. Watts retorted that the cadet corps was part of the military organization of the state and "being then thus in service of the state, the Confederate government had no authority to enforce into the Confederate service any one of the cadets." Watts further argued that cadets of the Lexington Military Academy in Virginia had been exempt from conscription and that the University of Alabama cadets stood in a like relationship with the Richmond authorities.[94]

In an attempt to convince the War Department, he invited the secretary of war to attend commencement exercises at the university on 14 July 1864 and to bring three Confederate army officers chosen by the secretary. They would study the situation at the university and make a public report in order that all might learn "what Alabama is doing in the military cause and

---

[94]Resolutions adopted 4 June 1863, by Board of Trustees of the University, in Watts Collection, ADAH; President L. C. Garland to Watts, 29 November 1864; Watts to General Jones M. Withers, 14 October 1864; James B. Sellers, *History of the University of Alabama* (University AL, 1953) 272; Watts to Seddon, 12 June 1864; Watts to Col. H. C. Lockhart, 3 May 1864.

what kind of young men she turns out for public service." Such a gesture, he added, "would show good faith on the part of the Confederacy." Neither Watts's letters nor the *Official Records* contain any evidence that the secretary of war even responded to this invitation.[95]

Another area of conflict between Watts and the Confederacy arose when Watts and conscription officials could not agree on which state civil officials were exempt from conscription. Although some disagreement occurred in all the Confederate states on this subject, Albert B. Moore, the authority on conscription in the Confederacy, declared that "the sharpest conflict over conscription of petty civil officers was in Alabama." The controversy revolved around the Confederate Exemption Law of 17 February 1864. The secretary of war interpreted it broadly so as to bring into the army many petty officials (justices of the peace, county commissioners, constables, police officers, etc.) whether they were elected before or after the law was passed. Watts asserted that many of these officials were essential to the operation of state government and were provided for under Alabama law, which he was sworn to uphold. He wrote Jones M. Withers, commander of the Confederate reserves for Alabama, "I learn that some of your enrolling officers have been taking by force officers of the State, holding not only my certificates, but those of Colonel Lockhart, commandant of conscripts. This state of things cannot long exist without a conflict between the Confederate and State authorities. I shall be compelled to protect my State officers with all the forces of the State at my command." General Withers's reply was polite but firm. He expressed a desire to "perpetuate the most frank and cordial co-operation" with the governor and asked Watts to furnish a list of his certified civil officials. He stated frankly that the situation could be changed only by a change of his orders from Richmond. Withers then sent his correspondence with Watts to Richmond with a cover letter in which he said, "I shall obey the orders given me, meeting force with force." As the dispute dragged on, Watts sent Secretary of War Seddon a hot ultimatum: "Unless you interfere," he warned, "there will be conflict between Confederate and State authorities. Officers of the State cannot be consribed [*sic*] without the consent of the State. . . . The police officers of Selma have been enrolled by force. These officers are indispensable to the administration of the State government." Seddon

---

[95]Watts to Seddon, 24 April 1864.

replied promptly: ''Officers of the State of Alabama, certified by you to be necessary to State administration, are exempt. Officers of the police of Selma are, I suppose, not considered as State officers. Cannot the courts decide? I only wish to enforce the laws, and deprecate conflict with the authorities of the State.'' He ended by telling Governor Watts that the issue scarcely entitled him to take up arms or to menace with resistance by force the administration of the department.[96]

The defense of Mobile remained a major problem for Watts as it had for his predecessors. Prior to Watts, more than 10,000 slaves had been impressed to build the defenses of the city. Yet shortly after his inauguration, Von Sheliha, Mobile's chief engineer, wrote the governor to ask for 4,000 slaves and 104 four-mule wagon teams to continue the work. The chief engineer informed the governor that the most essential fortifications could be completed in three months if sufficient labor and supplies could be obtained. The fortification of Mobile turned out to be an endless process. Much projected work was incomplete when Farragut ran his flotilla into the bay on 5 August 1864. The work was endless because the task was gargantuan—moving dirt by barge from one place to another in order to build redoubts and raise batteries to ring the city. Von Sheliha told Watts that in December 1863 he had only about 1,500 slaves working, which all but brought the work to a stop.[97]

Von Sheliha acknowledged the opposition of the planters to the impressment of slaves but said many of their complaints had now been met. Heated cabins, warm clothing, shoes, and medical care were now available to them and the government was making every effort not to keep the slaves for a longer time than that for which they had been impressed. Watts believed that much of the illness among the slaves at Mobile was a matter of getting acclimated and that longer terms of impressment would lower the incidence of illness. General Pillow and others suggested to the gov-

---

[96]Moore, *Conscription and Conflict*, 251-53; Watts to Jones M. Withers, in *OR,* ser. 4, vol. 3, 817; Watts to Seddon, 9 November 1864, ibid., 820; Withers to General S. Cooper, Adj. and Inspector General, 8 November 1864, ibid., 817-18; Withers to Watts, 8 November 1864, ibid. In addition to the police in Selma, the dispute concerned those in Mobile, members of the Board of Commissioners in Fayette County, and the nurses at the insane asylum, whom Watts acknowledged were not technically officers but were just as essential if the state was to continue to function.

[97]Von Sheliha to Watts, 13 December 1863, in *OR,* vol. 26, pt. 2, 501-504.

ernor that armies of several thousand slaves each be assembled to take turns of a year or more working at Mobile. The planters opposed longer terms than sixty days on any such system. Some of the most bitter and emotional letters in the governor's files were written to him by planters whose slaves had not been returned on time or whose slaves allegedly had been mistreated. The governor made a trip to Mobile early in his administration to check on conditions under which the impressed slaves lived and worked. He came back saying he was satisfied with the conditions.

In April 1864 opposition to the impressment of slaves and other property came to a head in Talladega County. The people held a mass meeting in the courthouse and appointed a committee, chaired by Lewis E. Parsons, to draw up resolutions petitioning the governor to intervene to stop any more impressments of slaves or teams from that county. They said the valley of the county where most of the food was grown had already furnished more than 700 slaves. They told the governor that they had made a pledge to the Talladega Hill County soldiers to feed their families—a pledge that they could not keep if any more slaves and teams were taken. To drive home the point, they declared that the soldiers would desert and come home if their families were not fed. Unlike Shorter, Watts always stressed that he was not in charge of impressment—that it was done by Confederate agents under Confederate law. The Talladega resolutions also complained about the cavalrymen and their consumption of the grain that could otherwise be used to feed the indigent families if the cavalry were withdrawn.[98]

Watts helped all he could but stopped short of getting personally involved in impressing the slaves as Shorter had. Yet he was fundamentally opposed to the impressment process and friction between him and the Confederate authorities occasionally came to the surface. Once he wrote to General Maury, commander at Mobile, ''You are well aware that the State of Alabama declined to make impressments after Congress gave the Confederate authorities the right to make them.'' He also told Maury that Von

---

[98]Ibid. Von Sheliha asked the governor to raise a corps of 5,000 Negro laborers to serve during the war. See Col. R. L. Pillow to Watts, 22 September 1864; Watts to John H. Dent, 14 April 1864. In his letter to Dent, Watts denied that he had impressed his slaves, told of his trip to Mobile, and argued that a longer period of impressment was needed for acclimation. For the Talladega meeting, see *OR,* vol. 33, pt. 3, 764-66; McMillan, *Alabama Confederate Reader,* 377-80.

Sheliha seemed to think the governor of Alabama was "only a high sheriff to execute the laws of Congress."[99]

As the Federal fleet and army began to close in on Mobile in the fall and winter of 1864, Watts and Confederate authorities expected a long siege of the city. Watts wrote Maury just after the Federal fleet got control of Mobile Bay, "I trust you will be able to hold Mobile, if not let it remain a heap of ashes before the Yankees pollute it with their footsteps." Watts thought it necessary to evacuate the women and children from the city. He said that they would be in the way of the fighting, that some of them would be needlessly killed, and that enough food could not be stored to feed them and the army in the event of a siege. The legislature provided for the evacuation inland and Watts directed the construction of houses to receive them. One such haven was built at Garland, near Greenville. Most of those evacuated, however, were cared for in the homes of inland citizens.[100]

It turned out that the siege did not last long. Although there are various explanations for what happened, apparently timing was the most important factor. It came when the war was all but over; the major Confederate armies had surrendered; the will to fight was gone; there was nothing left for which to fight.

In 1864 Jefferson Davis wanted more control of blockade-running. In April 1864 Watts joined Governor Brown of Georgia, Governor Zebulon Vance of North Carolina and Governor Charles Clark of Mississippi in signing a memorial against new Confederate regulations that required the states to give the Confederacy half of all space on blockade-runners owned in part or chartered by the states. To Watts this was just another form of impressment. In June 1864 the governors were able to get a bill through Congress overturning the regulations. President Davis vetoed the bill, arguing that only the Confederate government could regulate the trade for the good of the cause. He pointed out that some of the Confederate states had no port for blockade-running and emphasized that essential goods were needed—not luxury items. This issue became the main force behind the Conference of Confederate Governors which met in Augusta, Georgia, on 17 October 1864 to consult on this and other Confederate problems. Watts,

---

[99]Watts to General D. H. Maury, 16 August 1864, in *OR*, vol. 39, pt. 2, 780.

[100]Ibid.; Watts's Proclamation to Women of Mobile to Evacuate the City, in Moore, *Rebellion Record*, 8:44.

a prime mover in the original memorial against the regulations, attended the Augusta conference and supported the resolutions passed there—except one encouraging the use of Negro slaves in the Confederate army. He later told the Alabama legislature that he vehemently opposed such a move and would have voted against it at the conference, but was called home because of illness in his family before the matter came before the body.[101]

Tied to the blockade-running issue was the about-face of the Confederate government in regard to cotton trade. In 1864 the Confederacy began actively shipping cotton to Europe. Watts and other governors did not see why the states could not do the same. Alabama was sorely pressed to meet the interest on the state's debt in London and Watts wanted to use trade in cotton to meet the debt. There was also the matter of financing warm clothing and blankets for Alabama soldiers in cold Northern prisons, a matter that the legislature had mandated the governor to push forward. Watts wrote to President Davis asking permission to ship 1,000 bales of cotton through the lines to New York to finance the project. When the president gave his permission, Watts appointed Meyer Lehman, a Montgomery cotton-broker and sometime blockade-runner, and Isaac T. Tichenor, a Baptist minister, to carry out the mission, but they were refused a pass through the lines by U. S. Grant.[102]

Late in the war Watts was in touch with Andrew Magrath, the extreme states' rights governor of South Carolina, who sent ex-Governor John L. Manning of South Carolina to Montgomery in support of his plan to continue the war with state troops even though Richmond fell or the Confederacy surrendered. Magrath argued that the Confederacy was losing the war, not the states. He declared that reckless invasion of personal liberty and property rights by the Confederacy had dried up the will of the people to fight. Watts was in agreement that measures such as the impressment of goods and slaves and the tax-in-kind had greatly weakened the Confed-

---

[101]Memorial to the Confederate Congress signed by Watts, Brown, Vance, and Clark, in Montgomery *Daily Advertiser,* 30 June 1864; Coulter, *The Confederate States of America,* 293; Governor's message to legislature, November 1864, in Memphis *Daily Appeal,* 17 November 1864.

[102]*Acts of the Called and Fourth Regular Annual Session of the General Assembly of Alabama, 1864* (Montgomery, 1864) 63-65; Watts to Davis, 18 January 1865. See McMillan, *Alabama Confederate Reader,* 366-67, for Lehman and Tichenor's letter to Grant.

erate cause and turned the people against the government. While he did not commit himself to all of Magrath's proposals, he agreed that the "usurpation by the Confederacy" of many powers belonging to the states had weakened the war effort. Watts wrote Magrath that "many and grave errors have been committed by the President, his heads of departments, and Congress," but as to confronting Davis with remonstrances, he preferred that they be "confidential," at least for now. Magrath wanted Robert E. Lee made commander in chief of all the armies of the Confederacy and Joseph E. Johnston restored to his command. With regard to the latter, Watts wrote Magrath that he had already written the president asking for Johnston's restoral. Watts's personal feelings for the president would have kept him from asking Davis to give his powers of commander in chief to Lee. However, time was running out for Magrath and Watts. Magrath would soon flee from Sherman in Columbia, and Watts from Wilson in Montgomery.[103]

Despite Watts's states' rights stance as governor, he maintained cordial relations with President Davis. In fact, if Watts had not built personal ties with Davis while in his cabinet, he would have been much less cooperative with the Confederacy as governor. His personal friendship with Davis tended to check his states' rights proclivities. Davis wrote him a letter of regret when he resigned from the cabinet to become governor of Alabama, and their friendship lasted throughout their lives. When Davis spoke before the legislature of Alabama in September 1864, the Montgomery *Daily Mail* of 30 September 1864 reported that he paid "a glowing tribute to the capacity, gallantry, and patriotism of Governor Watts and urged upon the state and legislature the wisdom of his counsels."

This friendship withstood a poignant snub of General Bragg, Davis's special envoy, who was to confer with Watts in July 1864 on the military situation. When the general reached Montgomery, Watts wrote him a note saying the president had asked him to meet with Bragg, but "the frankness of my nature compels me to say that if I were to consult my private feelings alone, I should have no conference with you. But occupying the position of chief magistrate of one of the sovereign states of the Confederacy, I cannot permit personal considerations to interfere with the discharge of my

---

[103]Watts to Gov. Andrew G. Magrath of South Carolina, 13 February 1865; Watts to John L. Manning, 14 February 1865; Charles E. Cauthen, *South Carolina Goes to War, 1860-1865* (Chapel Hill, 1950) 227-28.

public duties.'' Bragg was insulted by the communication and left town without seeing the governor. Watts then wrote the president that if he [Davis] ever wanted to confer with him again, ''you will see the propriety of doing so through some other officer than General Bragg.'' President Davis turned Watts's letter over to Bragg for comment. Bragg wrote on the margin that Watts had ''deliberately tried to insult me'' and by doing so had ''degraded the high position of governor.'' In addition, Bragg charged that Watts was trying to make him the scapegoat ''in order to escape the withering criticism of his fellow citizens'' for the situation in which the governor found himself. Bragg was generally unpopular in many circles in Alabama at this time because of his alleged influence over Davis. However, much of Watts's animosity toward Bragg stemmed from the way Bragg and others had treated General James H. Clanton, whom Watts and Shorter defended as a fine army officer and disciplinarian, when a mutiny occurred in his army in south Alabama.[104] Although Shorter pleaded with Confederate authorities to send Clanton with his army to north Alabama, Clanton instead was stripped of his army and placed in command of about 200 cavalry in north Alabama.

Meanwhile, desertion was steadily increasing, especially in the Wiregrass and in northern Alabama, and public opinion made all legislation against harboring deserters a dead letter. In the winter of 1864-1865, a dinner was given in a Wiregrass town for fifty-seven deserters. Warrants were issued for their arrest at the dinner, but the arresting officer refused to serve them. Outlaw deserters burned the courthouse in Coffee County and murdered four of that county's best citizens. North Alabama was so infested with deserters that an officer sent to arrest them wrote Watts that in the thick woods ''you would as soon catch a flea'' as a deserter. Though the legislature promised to secure pardons for any deserter on his return to his unit, and though Watts pleaded with them to return, few complied.[105]

The growing number of sacrifices, the breakdown of authority, the drain on manpower, and dwindling hope of victory gradually brought the same

---

[104]President Davis to Watts, 18 July 1864; Watts to Braxton Bragg, 18 July 1864; Watts to President Davis, 30 July 1864. Bragg's notes on the margins of the latter letter, dated 18 August 1864, are all in the Manuscript Room, ADAH.

[105]McMillan, *Alabama Confederate Reader,* 380; Martin, *Desertion,* 145, 216-17, 233; Frank L. Owsley, ''Local Defense and the Overthrow of the Confederacy,'' *Mississippi Valley Historical Review* 11 (March 1925): 490.

desperate war weariness to Alabamians that was settling over much of the Confederacy. It seemed that the more the Davis and Watts administrations demanded of Alabamians, the more the defense of Alabama was neglected. By November 1864, the malaise that had long affected north and southeast Alabama in regard to the war was spreading to the rest of the state. Lieutenant Colonel H. C. Lockhart, commandant for conscription in Alabama, reported that desertion and a total disregard for orders from the War Department had spread to "some of the most wealthy and enlightened counties in the State." Among those named were Marengo, Greene, Sumter, Perry, and Dallas—all west-central Black Belt counties. He also reported:

> The unwillingness with which conscripts now take service in the Army, the tardiness with which men return to their command at the expiration of furloughs, and the presence of a very large and increasing number of deserters . . . as well as the great reluctance with which citizens respond to the call for the impressment or employment of slave labor, make it absolutely necessary that officers employed in the conscription service should be supplied with an adequate and effective force to enable them to enforce orders.[106]

Although Watts continued to appear optimistic in public meetings, he was well aware of his ineffectiveness and unpopularity by this time. He knew that he could not be reelected and apparently he did not want to try. Widespread speculation in the press indicated that Watts would decline to stand for reelection, and a letter to the governor said, "I am truly sorry you will not stand for reelection." A correspondent of the Columbus *Enquirer* in east Alabama was quoted in the Troy *Southern Advertiser* of 9 December 1864 as saying, "The people are organizing to cast about for a successor to Governor Watts." Watts wrote Governor Magrath of South Carolina that the legislature had twice refused to adopt his plans for a stronger militia and "I fear a new election shall place in power other men." There is little doubt that if the enemy had not occupied the heartland of Alabama and if the elections of August 1865 had taken place, the so-called

---

[106]H. C. Lockhart to Asst. Adj. General John C. Burch, 30 November 1864, in *OR*, ser. 4, vol. 3, 880-81.

Peace party would have gotten control of the government of Alabama and brought the whole military effort to an end.[107]

Military events moved swiftly in the state in the last few months of the war. Farragut captured Mobile Bay on 5 August 1864. The forts at the mouth of the bay were then vulnerable and soon fell to the enemy. Watts's determination could not save Alabama from defeat, and a letter from a citizen of Sparta was typical of those reaching the governor's desk at this time: "I regret that the people at home are not disposed to cooperate with you and no man can have their cooperation who undertakes at this day to put men in the service of their country." The writer added, "The people are using every effort to sustain the legislature [against you] because they have determined not to fight, though the Goths and Vandals are on them."[108]

The heartland of Alabama was destroyed by General James Wilson's raid in the spring of 1865. Wilson's 15,000 raiders wanted to destroy Selma's war works and the other industrial and mining sites and to occupy Forrest so that he could not help in the defense of Mobile. Wilson captured Selma, destroyed its immense war industry, and then turned toward Montgomery.[109]

The governor talked optimistically about the military situation until the very end. In an emergency meeting at the Montgomery Theatre on 25 February 1865, he said, "We hold more territory now than we did twelve months ago." When a voice from the audience disputed the statement, Watts called it the voice of "a croaker and Tory." He claimed that the Confederacy was stronger in munitions, supplies, and many other ways than at any time in the past, and he ended his remarks with the words of Patrick Henry: "Give me liberty or give me death." The governor's brave words could not stop the course of events and failed to compel the people to fight as Wilson moved even closer to Montgomery.[110]

---

[107]Reverend M. S. Andrews to Watts, 26 January 1865. See *Clarke County Journal*, 1, 9 February, 30 March 1865; Montgomery *Daily Mail*, 11 April 1865; Watts to Magrath, 13 February 1865. See also Frank L. Owsley, "Defeatism in the Confederacy," reprinted from the *North Carolina Historical Review* (July 1926): 1-13. The "Reconstructionists" were pushing M. J. Bulger of Tallapoosa County for governor.

[108]James L. Rushing to Watts, 20 October 1864.

[109]James Pickett Jones, *Yankee Blitzkrieg: Wilson's Raid through Alabama and Georgia* (Athens GA, 1976) 76-115.

[110]Montgomery *Daily Advertiser*, 3 March 1965, contains a synopsis of the theatre meeting of 25 February 1865.

Life went on as usual in the Governor's House. On April 4, the day after Richmond and Selma fell, the governor gave his daughter Kate in marriage to Robert M. Collins of West Point, Mississippi, a lawyer and Confederate soldier and the son of a Mississippian who owned seven plantations. Kate's bridal gown of ivory satin was brought to Montgomery through the blockade by Meyer Lehman, a blockade-runner and a friend of the family, at a cost of $700. Since railroads were unavailable, the couple made their way to West Point in a magnificent carriage drawn by matching bay horses in silver-mounted harness. On this trip they learned that Lee had surrendered. Everywhere around them their way of life was coming to an end.[111]

Watts maintained an air of optimism as Wilson's troops approached Montgomery from Selma. He seemed like the main actor in a drama that was not real. He proclaimed, "The military authorities here are determined to defend the city. With my consent, the seat of government shall not be surrendered as long as there is a reasonable hope of defending it." He told the militia: "If you will come we can save our state. Without delay,the commanders of several counties east and south of the Alabama River, will send their men to this place." Nevertheless, an exodus of civilians began and meetings between civil and military authorities were marked by confusion. Apparently Richard Taylor, commander of the military district of Alabama, Mississippi, and East Louisiana, made the decision not to defend the city. However, the Greensboro *Alabama Beacon* of 21 April 1865 reported that "Governor Watts, finding that he could not muster troops enough to make a successful resistance determined several days before the enemy reached the city to give it up and, as we have understood, so advised the citizens."[112]

Before Wilson reached Montgomery, Watts left by rail with at least some of the state archives for Columbus, Georgia, whence he proceeded downriver to Eufaula, which the governor had decided to make the seat of government for the emergency. The city of Montgomery was surrendered by Mayor W. L. Coleman and the city council, who were very anxious that

---

[111]Account of the wedding of Kate Prudence Watts and Robert M. Collins, 3 April 1865, in Watts Papers, ADAH. Internal criticism dates the manuscript sometime after 1915.

[112]Proclamation of Gov. Watts, 4 April 1865; Montgomery Daily *Advertiser,* 18 April 1865; *Alabama Beacon,* 21 April 1865.

Wilson's forces not "sack and burn" the city as in Selma. They were given assurances of protection for its inhabitants while the raiders moved through the area.

On 24 April the Montgomery *Daily Mail* reported the governor was back in Montgomery, giving out the latest war news. He then went with a friend, the Reverend M. N. Eley, to Union Springs where remnants of the Confederate military forces were concentrating. There, on 1 May 1865 he was arrested by Union General T. J. Lucas and sent to Major General A. J. Smith in Montgomery for his disposal. Apparently he was then sent to Macon, Georgia, and detained for only a short time. The Montgomery *Mail* of 19 June 1865 quoted a Northern paper as saying that "Governor Watts who was arrested a few days ago at Macon, Georgia has been released and has returned to Montgomery."[113]

Governor Watts lived some twenty-seven years after the war ended, dying in 1892 at the age of seventy-four. He lost his property at the end of the war; Federal troops burned his cotton, his plantation home and his slave houses. His investment in nearly 200 slaves was also gone. He was forced into bankruptcy as he was liable for some $100,000 in debts—two-thirds of which were security for other people. Before his death he paid all the debt and became a man of some wealth again.

Watts was an ardent Confederate veteran and never tired of extolling the virtues of the men who fought in gray. He made a major address when Jefferson Davis came to Montgomery in 1887 to dedicate the monument to the soldiers of the Confederacy. Davis paid his respects to him as "cabinet member, soldier, statesman and patriotic governor." After the war, Watts became a Conservative Democrat, supporting nominees of that party for governor and its candidates for president. He was elected to office only one time after the war—to the legislature from Montgomery County in 1880. He had played an earlier role in the overthrow of Radical Reconstruction. Watts wanted to be United States senator after the war, but the opportunity never came. He also aspired to be a member of Grover Cleveland's cabinet. Watts was one of the leading lawyers in Alabama in the

---

[113]Letter of G. F. Eley to the editor of the Montgomery *Advertiser*, 15 October 1933. Eley said that as a boy of fifteen he witnessed Watts's arrest at his father's house in Union Springs. See also Brigadier General T. J. Lucas to Major S. L. Woodward, Cavalry forces, Dept. of the Gulf, 23 June 1865, in *OR*, vol. 49, pt. 1, 305-307.

years after the war, with a greater practice before the Alabama Supreme
Court than any other man at the time. His death on 16 September 1892 was
unexpected, although he had collapsed with a heart attack the day before.
He was buried in Oakwood Cemetery in Montgomery. His epitaph reads:
"Lawyer, Soldier, Statesman, Patriot. He loved his state and its people,
his people loved and honored him."[114]

---

[114]Watts's postbellum career is treated at length in *Representative Men of the South*, 52-
70.

Alienation from the Confederacy

Alienation from the Confederacy, which became so evident after July 1863, had spread to all the shaded areas of Alabama by 1864, and after the Battles of Franklin and Nashville in late 1864, began to spread to the unshaded areas.

Chapter IV

AN APPRAISAL

The appraisal of Alabama's Civil War governors must answer the questions: How much did each contribute to the success—and ultimate failure—of the Confederacy? Which of the many problems plaguing the governors caused the most damage in the collapse of the home front? Of the three governors, John Gill Shorter gave the most cooperation to the Confederate war effort. Andrew Barry Moore held back guns that the Confederacy needed at the beginning of the war. Ironically, Thomas H. Watts, who upheld the central powers of the Confederacy while serving as attorney general in Jefferson Davis's cabinet, became an ardent states' righter and thus an obstructionist to many Confederate policies while serving as governor. Who was the best governor? There is no easy answer. Each was in power at a different stage of the war and met the issues in his own way. None were guilty of evading their duties.

Governor Moore moved with precision and speed through the secession crisis. This included the calling of the secessionist convention, the appointment of commissioners to other Southern states, the seizure of Federal forts and the donation of military aid to Pensacola at the request of the governor of Florida even before the passage of Alabama's ordinance of secession. Cooperationists denounced his activities in the secession crisis as ruthless and unconstitutional and the Federal government did not forget

charges against him. After four years of war he was the only one of Alabama's governors to be imprisoned. Moore worked tirelessly as aide to
Governor Shorter and helped Governor Watts to feed thousands of starving Alabamians in the last years of the war. His dedication to Alabama was
not limited to his term as governor but endured until his death. Because of
Moore's role as secessionist governor, students of Alabama history have
not recognized the artful skills he displayed in keeping the Democratic party
together prior to John Brown's raid at Harpers Ferry. Prior to 1859 few
Democrats in Alabama did as much to uphold the national wing of the
Democratic party in the state.

John Gill Shorter was perhaps the most conscientious and dedicated of
Alabama's Civil War governors. A devout Baptist, he believed with John
Calvin that he was elected by God and, as he told the people in the election
of August 1863, he had an "inward approval" that neither defeat nor victory could deny him. The people soundly defeated him, but his convictions
enabled him to take the loss without faltering. He was not a politician, but
his minority reports from legislative committees indicated that he was a
"man of principle." Shorter understood the difficulties that the Confederacy faced regarding conscription. He told the secretary of war that the
war could only be won by "men of deep devotion to liberty. If we are to
depend upon [conscription] to maintain the liberty of the South, I should
almost despair of our ultimate triumph." Shorter used his office to impress
slave labor and thus lost the support of many of his fellow planters.

Affable and genial "Big Tom" Watts was the last war governor. He
was waiting in the shadows and had wanted to be governor from almost
the beginning of the war. He would rather be governor of the "sovereign
state of Alabama" than be attorney general of the Confederacy, but he
served as both. As attorney general, he was a nationalist or centralist, but
as governor he became an ardent advocate of the states' rights of Alabama.
Thus he was an obstructionist in the war effort. Watts objected to many
Confederate policies but was probably never more correct in gauging the
results than when he opposed impressment of private property. "If we fail
to achieve our independence in this war," he warned, "failure will arise
over our breaking down the spirits of the people. . . . Impressment of
property only aggravates the price of goods and creates opposition to the
government and our own cause." The motivation for Watts's reversal from
Confederate nationalist to states' rights advocate remains puzzling. When
he became governor during the most difficult part of the war, he was more

concerned with his state's problems than with constitutional theory. Of the three wartime governors, Watts was the most gifted speaker and possessed a superior intellect. He was one of the most able jurists of nineteenth-century Alabama. He never felt more comfortable than when making a speech or arguing a case in court. In political life today, he would probably be described as charismatic. As Alabama's second native-born governor and a former Whig in 1863, he was the only man of that party to ever be elected governor of Alabama. Watts was fated to be placed in the most tragic situation of all. To the very end he talked of victory and called on the militia though the legislature had denied him its control. He remained calm. As the walls of the state and the Confederacy fell around him, he acted as if 3 April 1865 was a normal day and even gave his daughter Kate in marriage to a planter's son from Mississippi. Selma and Richmond had fallen the day before. In several days Watts fled from Montgomery to avoid capture by General James Harrison Wilson and to establish a new capital for the state in Eufaula. Sadly, he soon realized there was no need for a new capital. Alabama's resistance had completely collapsed.

All of Alabama's Civil War governors were quite capable but none of them possessed the political wizardry that would have been required to please the wartime electorate in Alabama. As members of the cotton aristocracy, they were all under suspicion from the start. They had an economic interest in the outcome of the war. All were slaveholders. Watts was the largest slaveholder at the secessionist convention. They belonged to the lawyer-planter class and were politically vulnerable to charges made against that class during the war—such as that the war was a ''rich man's war and a poor man's fight.'' All were identified in the public mind with those who benefited from the unpopular exemption clauses of the conscription acts. Less than ten percent of Alabama's white population belonged to the large planter class of the governors; eighty percent or more of the white population were small farmers, small planters who worked in the fields with their slaves, and poor whites. Alabama's three Civil War governors were unable to do what Joseph E. Brown, of poor-white ancestry, did in Georgia—that is, to consistently get majority support at the ballot box during the war. But although Alabama held its wartime governors to one term, this was typical in most Confederate states. Brown was able to rise above this convention. Georgia was the only Confederate state where a governor was able to dominate the scene as completely as Brown did. In North Carolina, Zebulon Vance, considered with Brown one of the Confederacy's two strongest governors, did manage to win a second term in 1864, but John Willis Ellis was also governor of North Carolina until his death in July 1861 while in office. All Confederate states had two or more governors during the war except Georgia and Tennessee. In Tennessee this occurred because people were not free to make this decision.

Intense and long-existing sectionalism (based on economic interests and lack of transportation between north and south Alabama) also caused a lack of unity in Alabama during the Civil War. None of the wartime governors could satisfy both north and south Alabama—especially after the occupation of the northernmost part of the state in April 1862. Even the political genius, Joseph E. Brown, did not have to face his people in an election after part of his state had been occupied by the enemy as Shorter did. It is questionable whether a governor from the northern part of the state could have brought more unity to the state in the war period. The people of north Alabama would probably have been more cooperative in the war effort, but it is likely that the results would have been the same. We will never really know. Prior to 1850 northern Alabama produced a disproportionately large share of governors. After that time southern Alabama emerged as the dominant section and was able to nominate and elect its sons throughout the war period.

South Alabama took the state out of the Union in 1861. The war came and northern Alabama, the cooperationist part of the state, was invaded in April 1862—thus becoming the first part of Alabama to suffer the horrors of civil war. These events produced volatile and turbulent politics in Alabama during the war that none of the governors could moderate or control. Northern Alabama leaders kept demanding that the enemy be driven out, but the state had neither the arms nor the manpower to accomplish this. Shorter supported the Confederate policy of consolidating troops in Virginia and the West. He pointed out that if the Confederacy won the war, the northern Alabama situation would take care of itself. "Friends of Watts" made the consolidation policy an issue in the election of 1863, but after Watts's election little was heard of the issue from his camp.

The "final straw" for the home front came in Shorter's second year in office. Home-front difficulties were multiplying before July 1863. After Gettysburg and Vicksburg a defeatist attitude set in that could not be reversed in spite of how Shorter—or later Watts—might try. Home-front problems became acute during Shorter's last year in office and his inability to solve them was a major reason for his defeat in the August 1863 election. These matters reached crisis proportions during Watts's eighteen months in office—and remained that way because there was no way to alleviate them, nor an avenue for peace to eliminate them. The degree to which Alabama's governors had to struggle with these difficulties forms an index to the decline of the ability to fight the war in Alabama from 1863 until the collapse in April 1865. Paralysis would have come much sooner under the proper circumstances. That came in April 1865 with the arrival of the Federal army.

There were many problems that weakened and finally caused the collapse of the home front. They included: opposition to conscription and wanton desertion; desertion by otherwise conscientious soldiers because of the sufferings of their families at home; disorders in half the Alabama counties resulting from desertion; the inability of the government, despite heroic efforts, to feed and clothe the destitute; a breakdown of the democratic election process; hunger and suffering in many parts of the state that exceeded human endurance; transportation problems that prevented the distribution of food and other essentials; sectional discord between north and south Alabama, especially after the Federal occupation of Alabama north of the Tennessee River in April 1862; the refusal of the legislature to effectively reorganize the militia and place it under the control of the governors; the impressment of property without just compensation; the onerous tax-in-kind; inflation and extortion; the scarcity of cards for making cloth at home; and the scarcity of salt for curing and preserving meat. Alabama's wartime governors struggled with all of these problems, but they failed to resolve any of them before the civilian population became so demoralized that it no longer could provide for itself or the army. These problems were so devastating that when the Federal army arrived in the Alabama heartland in the spring of 1865, it only had to occupy Alabama rather than conquer it.

The subject of desertion from the army requires further exploration because it became the main cause of the collapse of the home front. Desertions occurred for all kinds of reasons, many frivolous and base, but the one that public opinion in Alabama almost universally condoned was desertion of a soldier because his family was near starvation or was being mistreated at home—especially by outlaws or bushwhackers. Protecting and preserving one's family was deemed a higher and more sacred obligation than fighting for one's country.

The results of desertion were twofold. First, it weakened Confederate armies and caused them to lose battles they might have otherwise won. Second and more immediately, good citizens and soldiers who deserted to protect their families were lumped together with those who deserted for base reasons and treated as outlaws or bushwhackers. All were outside the law after deserting and thus were forced to become bushwhackers to sustain themselves and their families. They preyed on their neighbors and laid the country to waste. This caused more of the good men to return home and further increased societal disorganization. Thus, desertion begot more desertion and as the war continued more of the state was laid to waste and taken out of the war.

Desertion and opposition to conscription were initially based on disillusionment with the system or the status quo. Many people in northern Alabama never really accepted secession or the creation of the Confederacy—not even in the first months of the war as earlier writers have claimed. In the summer of 1861 letters to Governor Moore bear witness to the fact that Unionists or other opponents of Confederates were contesting the state's decision to secede in eight northwest Alabama counties. They were organizing themselves into units for protection and parading with the American flag, some of them accompanied by drummer boys. They felt that secession had not been fairly or legally accomplished because it had not been submitted to the people for their approval or rejection.

Those protesting secession in northern Alabama in 1861 were poor whites and small farmers, but in 1862 many prominent men in that part of the state also began to show their Union colors. In the same year C. C. Sheats of Winston County was expelled from the legislature because of "complicity with the enemy." After occupation, Huntsville became notorious for its treason and many public men were implicated throughout northern Alabama. Ex-United States senator Jeremiah Clemens, a cooperationist whom Governor Moore had made major general of the Alabama Militia in an effort to secure his loyalty, went over to the enemy. Many northern Alabamians spoke openly in favor of the Union and some went north behind Union lines.

The first deserters rallied around the pro-Union mountain sections of northern Alabama and the poor counties of the Wiregrass near the Florida line. In both cases the Federals were only a short distance away. The Federals never lost Fort Pickens in Pensacola harbor and after April 1862 they controlled Alabama north of the Tennessee River. From their nearby positions, deserters became the "eyes and ears" of the Federal army and were often in communication with them. Anti-Confederate sentiment was so prevalent in northern Alabama that Union forces recruited a whole regiment of troops in 1862-1863 from its hills.

As the war lengthened and desertion became more prevalent, the Confederacy depended more heavily on the states to control it. The deserters were better armed than the troops Alabama governors sent against them because they left the Confederate army with their guns and all the ammunition they could carry. The Confederacy lost small arms and ammunition to deserters and was unable to replace them. The old story about the deserter who, when asked for his furlough papers, patted his gun and said, "This is my furlough," has been told so many times that it has become trite; but it depicts the situation adequately. In the last two years of the war the state had few arms. Governor Shorter attempted to manufacture arms through large state subsidies to small munitions works, but this was not productive. Eight thousand Mississippi rifles contracted for at least a year before could not be delivered on 1 May 1863. Josiah Gorgas worked miracles in producing arms in the Ordnance Bureau of the Confederacy, but the plants in Selma could rarely spare arms and ammunition for state troops. The state had fewer arms in 1863-1864 than in 1861-1862 because the purchases at the beginning of the war had eventually been used to arm volunteers as they went into the Confederate army.

If Confederate forces were sent against deserters, they were usually units of the Confederate cavalry, some of which became almost as corrupt as the deserter bands in the latter part of the war. The infantry was tied down by the fighting on the Virginia and Western fronts and could not be moved fast enough to catch deserters in their various hiding places. Hence the Confederate cavalry was used to hunt deserters. This cavalry became notorious for its plundering. It was often hard to tell whether mounted men who appeared in a community were deserters or the Confederate cavalry. When the people are as afraid of their own forces as they are of deserter bands, society has disintegrated to a hopeless state. It is understandable that many joined peace societies and dreamed of the restoration of the old Union. Under the circumstances the Federal Union was remembered as an idealized friend and the Confederacy was viewed as the enemy. Many people longed for a return to the prosperity, peace, and security they had known before 1861 in the old Union.

By 1863 deserters had disorganized society and paralyzed its ability to function in a wartime economy in large sections of Alabama. In June of that year Gideon J. Pillow's Bureau of Conscription reported that there were 8,000 to 10,000 "deserters and tory conscripts" in the mountains of north Alabama. In the same month the assistant quartermaster general notified Quartermaster General A. C. Myers that disorders resulting from desertion were so prevalent in eight north Alabama counties, five counties in southeast Alabama, and one county in southwest Alabama that it would be impractical to attempt collecting the tax-in-kind in those counties.[1] By February of 1865 half the counties in the state were in a similar condition as the following report to the secretary of war reveals. Speaking of Hood's Army of Tennessee after its defeat at Nashville, Jones M. Withers, commanding the Confederate reserves in Alabama, wrote:

> The tone of public sentiment in this State is most lamentably despondent. The old Unionists and reconstructionists . . . have seized on late reverses and been most active in charging them all on the President as their author, in having removed General Johnston. The straggling, scattered, undisciplined, disorganized condition and consequent lawless conduct of the Army of Tennessee in passing through the State has unfortunately added much to the success of disloyal efforts to increase despondency, spread discontent, and organize opposition to the Government and to the continuance of the war. Deserters and stragglers by the hundreds are now scattered broadcast throughout this State and such is the state of public sentiment that in half the counties in the State they can remain with impunity.[2]

Since the peace society did not keep records and reportedly did not elect officials, little is known about the organization. It is known that their membership grew and prospered in the areas of Alabama dominated by deserters. They preferred to remain mysterious under the general name "peace society," although we know that on occasion other nomenclature was used in referring to them. A Virginian writing in 1863 about the organization referred to them as the "Washington Constitutional Union" in Alabama.[3]

---

[1]Assistant Quartermaster General Larkin Smith to Quartermaster General A. C. Myers, 19 June 1863, *OR,* ser. 4, vol. 2, 575-76.

[2]Jones M. Withers to Secretary of War John C. Breckinridge, 7 February 1865, *OR,* ser. 4, vol. 3, 1064-65.

[3]Edward Younger, ed., *Inside the Confederate Government: The Diary of Robert Garlick Hill Kean* (New York, 1957) 73.

In the same year John Clisby of Coosa County, writing to Governor Shorter, used the term "peace society."[4] He said that the movement in northern Alabama was "open, bold, and defiant. Their earnest desire is not for independence but reunion." Since it kept no records, there is no indication of how large the society became in Alabama. Walter L. Fleming, in his "The Peace Movement in Alabama during the Civil War," has estimated that at least half of the men left on the home front became members.[5]

In December 1863 the first startling revelation about the damage the society was causing in the army came when sixty to seventy soldiers in General James H. Clanton's brigade at Pollard mutinied by laying down their arms and refusing to fight. Nearly all of Clanton's brigade were from the poorer classes of southeastern Alabama, where desertion and opposition to the war was common. The home influence on them was strong—with nearly all their homes less than a hundred miles away. With encouragement from the people of their own section who were members of the peace society, they took an oath among themselves "never to fight the enemy, to desert, and to encourage desertion." They also pledged that they would do all they could to defeat the Confederacy and end the war. Seventy of the soldiers were arrested and sent to Mobile to stand trial before a court-martial. The court-martial found that few of the men had joined the army for treasonable purposes, but Clanton was blamed for lack of discipline among his troops by Joseph E. Johnston and others. Clanton, Governor Watts, ex-Governor Shorter, and others asked that troops that were relocated from their homes be sent to northern Alabama because they were so badly needed there. However, the troops were scattered among the armies in the west. Clanton was convinced that the loss of his troops represented a continued persecution of him by General Bragg.[6]

In late 1864 there were clandestine meetings in northern Alabama between General P. D. Roddey, other Confederates, and the local Federal authorities, all of whom wanted peace. Scanty references to these meetings in the *Official Records* reveal plans to approach Governor Watts on the subject and get his cooperation if possible. If they did not get his cooperation, they would run a peace candidate against him in the August 1865

---

[4]John Clisby to Governor John Gill Shorter, 22 July 1863.

[5]In *South Atlantic Quarterly* 2 (1903): 254-55.

[6]McMillan, *The Alabama Confederate Reader*, 392-93.

election. They planned to take immediate control over the government after they won instead of waiting for the installation of a new administration.[7]

As the state struggled to prevent economic collapse—to support the army and civilian population—a revolution in economic affairs occurred. Regulation of private property and society in the interest of public welfare became common. In 1861 the legislature took the unusual step of passing a law forbidding the shipment of salt out of the state. When a company tried to ship salt out before the law went into effect, Governor Moore ordered its seizure. When the owners of the *Florida,* a merchant ship in Mobile Bay, would not allow its conversion into a gunboat under lease to the state, Moore seized the vessel, leaving payment to a board of appraisers. In April 1862 Shorter used his executive power to stop the manufacture of grain into liquor in order to preserve the grain supply for bread to feed the hungry. In December of that year the legislature placed the whole distilling business under the regulation of the governor, requiring a license from him for the manufacture of whiskey for medicinal and war purposes. In 1862 Shorter also leased the lower salt works in Clarke County to Figh and Company. All salt produced was assigned to the indigent families of soldiers from the state. The governor then decided to build a state salt manufacturing plant at the upper salt works in Clarke County and this venture was very successful. Shorter knew that he did not immediately need salt, but he used state funds to purchase a lease at the springs in Saltville, Virginia, which he placed in the charge of a Knoxville, Tennessee, company. This company would supply salt to indigent families of soldiers in north Alabama. In December 1862 the legislature passed—and Shorter signed into law—an act to abolish speculation in corn. Anyone selling corn except the producer had to get a license from the probate judge in the county of sale, which limited the seller to a profit of twenty percent or less under penalty of a $500 fine and six months in jail.

The legislature under both Shorter and Watts appropriated huge sums to keep the indigent families of soldiers from starvation—$5 million under Shorter and another $8 million under Watts. The larger sum under Watts indicates that the problem grew much larger during his eighteen months in office. The courts of county commissioners, city councils, and private

---

[7]J. J. Giers to Lt. General U. S. Grant, 26 January 1865, *OR,* ser. 1, vol. 49, pt. 1, 590-91. See also Frank L. Owsley, "Defeatism in the Confederacy," *North Carolina Historical Review* 3 (July 1926): 13-15.

charities raised more money for the purpose. But problems with drought, inflation, extortion, and transportation caused the state to be only partially successful in maintaining the indigent. Desertion rates continued to grow. Watts said in March 1864 that "the cries of starving people" were coming to him every day from north Alabama. When the war closed, the state was furnishing bread and salt to some 139,000 people.[8]

The state appropriations were provided by simply printing more paper money, which in turn brought further inflation. The complete disintegration of finances in the Confederacy has long been recognized as a reason for the collapse of the home front and defeat of the state's armies. Shorter tried so hard to regulate the economy in the interest of all the people that he probably expected some reward for his efforts at the polls in August 1863. However, a ground swell from the poor in his favor failed to materialize. In Georgia, Joseph E. Brown's popularity came in part from helping the poor and the downtrodden. Shorter did not receive the same benefits from working incessantly to supply bread and salt to Alabamians.

In addition to regulating the economy in the interest of public welfare, the state of Alabama subsidized or manufactured guns, shoes for Alabama troops, and other war materials on a large scale. On 7 December 1861 the legislature made an appropriation of $250,000 that it directed the governor to spend on encouraging the manufacture of firearms. The same act appropriated another $50,000 to encourage the manufacture of powder, saltpeter, sulphur, and lead. With this money, Shorter made large subsidies to small munitions companies for the manufacture of guns and other war supplies. The legislature also appropriated $250,000 for the manufacture or purchase of 50,000 pairs of shoes for Alabama soldiers in the Confederate army. The law gave power to impress with just compensation all leather and other materials necessary to bring the project to a successful conclusion. The governor was able to get the delivery of the shoes on time, but his munitions orders arrived late or not at all. The legislature appropriated $60,000 for the purchase or manufacture of cotton and wool cards that both Shorter and Watts used for domestic manufacturing and overseas purchases. Watts was more successful in running cards through the blockade, but neither governor was able to appreciably reduce the shortage.

The most significant result of placing the state government in business on a large scale during the war was that it reopened a long struggle in the

---

[8]*American Encyclopedia* (New York, 1865) 16.

state's history. The controversy went back to the 1820s when Governor Israel Pickens created the state bank. The bank became corrupt and lost much of the state's money, especially money set aside for education. With this scandal in the background, Governor John Winston in the 1850s vetoed all bills granting state aid to railroads—contending that the state should stay out of business. The legislature sustained his vetoes, and he became known as the "veto governor." This issue provides an excellent example of the history of one era affecting another. The entry of the state into business during the Civil War prepared the way for Radicals to spend millions on railroad building in the state during Reconstruction—thus bankrupting the state.

The manner in which elections were conducted in Alabama during the war also contributed to the collapse of the home front. The people were witnesses to a complete breakdown of the democratic process. The breakdown began when the secessionists would not allow the people a referendum on the issue of secession. The Democratic party contributed to the debacle in 1861 when they abandoned nominating conventions, platforms, and open debate on the issues. They mistakenly thought that political divisions could be set aside for the duration of the war in the interest of unity. The Democrats followed this course for two reasons. First, they were afraid to reopen the secession issue so soon after the decision was made to secede. Second, they reasoned that it would be too partisan for the Democrats to go through the party political cycle of nominating conventions, and so on, when the opposition party was too weak to do so. This act of self-denial exuded a false patriotism. They did not want the people to decide; it was their way of saying: "Let sleeping dogs lie." The people's right to know and to make decisions was violated. It is understandable that north Alabama yeomanry, in their first protests against secession, longed for the Jacksonian democracy of the 1830s and 1840s. They had lost an inalienable right to control their own destiny by deciding issues at the voting places.

The pattern in regard to holding elections during the war was set when the Democrats handled the gubernatorial election as they did in August 1861—that is, the newspapers nominated the candidates and the people decided on one of them in the general election. In the interest of unity, there was no debate or discussion by the candidates. The people could only guess the position of the candidates on the issues. This decision did more damage to the democratic process in 1863 than in 1861. In 1863 there were many issues raised by the war; in 1861 there were few issues unless the question of secession was placed under review. Despite Democratic fears, this was unlikely so soon after the decision to secede. In 1863 Watts chose not to campaign and turned out to be a "war man all over." Thus a situation had developed where the voters wanted to wind down the war but elected someone who wanted to do just the opposite. They were understandably disillusioned with a system that had placed them in such a mess. Many Alabamians gave up any hope of deciding issues at the ballot box and instead increasingly joined the peace movement or resorted to guerrilla and other such tactics outside the system. The very foundations of the home front throughout the state were shaken by this lack of democratic process. The people lost the will to fight. They longed for the reestablishment of the old Union to save them from the new despotism that took their property without compensation, conscripted them and forced them to fight against their will—a government whose policies had brought about a reign of terror in half the counties in Alabama. The vast majority of the people had reached the conclusion that there was no reason to continue a war that the Confederacy had already lost—except to save slavery from extinction and they were not slaveholders.

By August 1863 the home front in Alabama was in turmoil. Large numbers of people wanted peace and reconstruction but did not know how to get them. Thousands on the home front (the army could not vote) voted for Thomas H. Watts, the old Whig, because he represented a possibility for change (if not for peace and security, he might at least get them out of the desperate situation they were in). Many of Watts's votes were cast by wishful thinkers—any candidate who openly campaigned for peace in 1863 would have taken thousands of Watts's votes, thus drastically reducing his majority. However, they were forced to choose between the longtime secessionist, John Gill Shorter, and the old Whig, Thomas H. Watts, who had decided at the eleventh hour that Lincoln's election justified secession. The voters felt the choice was clear—it had to be Watts. Watts's uncharted course offered hope; Shorter's offered more of the same war miseries. In other words, in the Alabama election of August 1863 the electorate knew too much about Shorter; they knew too little about Watts. It may be argued that the voters were simpleminded to think that a man from Jefferson Davis's own cabinet might bring peace to Alabama. This is not true—they were merely human beings trapped in an unbearable situation from which they were trying to extricate themselves.

In the selection of legislators in 1863, the electorate chose their neighbors, men who represented their true feelings. These men had not participated in the agitation that brought on the war and they reflected the people's desire to end the war and secure the most acceptable peace terms. They were convinced that the Confederacy was defeated and they saw no reason for further sacrifice of life and property. Unfortunately, the lack of an open campaign in which the gubernatorial candidates could express themselves caused a "war man" to be elected governor. The resulting situation tied the state government in knots for the duration of the war—which manifested itself in the repeated refusal of the legislature to give the governor control of the militia. Alabama and the Confederacy limped toward defeat with thousands of the militiamen under the control of neither the governor nor the Confederacy. Disorders were occurring everywhere, and Federal armies were marching through the state. Most of the militiamen were in the first class and therefore tied to their counties of residence. Thus the governor could not concentrate them effectively. An energetic new governor was elected in August 1863, but from that day onward the legislature and the people were dragging their feet to the finish. A new day arrived when the legislature filled the two open seats in the Confederate Senate, formerly occupied by William L. Yancey and C. C. Clay, with two co-operationists of 1861—Robert Jemison and Richard Wilde Walker. Thomas H. Watts, the new governor, wanted to press on with the war. He made appeals and exhorted the legislature and the people to perform their duties, but his entreaties fell on deaf ears. In one of his final appeals, Watts pleaded with the militia to offer themselves on a voluntary basis to defend Montgomery in April 1865, but they did not respond. The people refused to continue the struggle. The war was over in Alabama.

BIBLIOGRAPHY

PRIMARY SOURCES

Manuscripts

Governors' Letters

The most important sources for this monograph are the letters and papers of three Civil War governors. The letters that the governors wrote are copied in ledger books of the day and are easily read because in this period a good secretary had to excel in penmanship, and penmanship was an important course in all schools and colleges. The letters to the governors are a different matter. They were written on all kinds of paper, which has often faded along with the homemade ink of the period—making them very hard to read. Both spelling and sentence structure reflect widespread illiteracy in the State. These are loose letters—not arranged in any order at the time they were used by the writer. The important point is that so many of them have been preserved, and with diligence most of them can be deciphered by the scholar.

Although there are over 1,000 letters in each governor's collection, the number in each case reflects the course of the war—the Moore collection having the least because he served less than a year after the war began and this was before many problems and burdens of the people became apparent. The Shorter collection has many more items because he served two full years and the war had become very unpopular before he gave way to Watts. The Watts collection is the largest because the problems and burdens of the people had become unbearable by his time, even though the war ended at least four months before his two-year term had run its course.

These letters are the most important source for portraying the major thesis of this study: when federal armies reached central and southern Alabama in late 1864 and early 1865, they only had to occupy the state—not conquer it. Society and government in the state had completely collapsed and were in a state of paralysis.

Although some of the letters to and from the governors are printed in the *War of the Rebellion Records,* this correspondence is always between the governors and important Alabamians (congressmen, generals, and Confederate officials) and never the correspondence of the common man. It is the latter that so vividly portrays conditions on the home front.

Governor Andrew Barry Moore Collection of Letters and Papers, 1858-1861.

Governor John Gill Shorter Collection of Letters and Papers, 1861-1863.

Governor Thomas Hill Watts Collection of Letters and Papers, 1863-1865.

Governors' Proclamation Book

This book was kept by the secretary of state, but many of the governors' proclamations are not recorded therein. The three governors issued several hundred proclamations during the war. A complete file can only be pieced together by using the proclamation book, each governor's own personal papers, and the newspapers where one or more proclamations ran a number of times every month of the year. At no other time in the State's history has the proclamation been so important in dispensing information, directing Alabama's efforts in the war, and calling on the people for every sacrifice. As the war effort faltered and then failed, these proclamations show the increasing desperation of the executive branch of the government.

Governor Moore's Order Book

Apparently because he wanted to avoid publicity, Moore placed his early orders in a small ledger book and did not send them to the secretary of state.

Miscellaneous

Manuscript Census of Alabama, 1850—Agricultural and Slave Schedules.

Manuscript Census of Alabama, 1860—Agricultural and Slave Schedules.

Manuscript Journal of the Called Session 1864 and the Fourth Annual Session of the House of Representatives of the State of Alabama 1864.

Published Diaries, Letters, Memoirs, and Papers

Chesnut, Mary Boykin. *Mary Chesnut's Civil War.* Edited by C. Vann Woodward. New Haven: Yale University Press, 1981.

"Correspondence of T. R. R. Cobb, 1860-1862." *Publications of the Southern Historical Association* 11 (May 1907): 159-83.

Friends of Watts. "Hand Bill on Election of August, 1863." Watts Papers. Alabama Department of Archives and History.

Moore, Frank. *The Rebellion Record; Diary of American Events, with Documents, Narratives, Incidents, Poetry, etc.* 11 vols. New York: G. P. Putnam, 1861-1863; D. Van Nostrand, 1864-1868.

Rowland, Dunbar, ed. *Jefferson Davis, Constitutionalist: His Letters, Papers and Speeches.* 10 vols., Little and Ives Company, 1923.

Smith, William R. *The History and Debates of the Convention of the People of Alabama, January 1861.* Atlanta: Rice and Company, 1861.

Taylor, Richard. *Destruction and Reconstruction.* Edited by Richard B. Harwell. New York: Longmans Green and Company, 1955.

Official Documents

Federal

U.S. War Department. *The War of the Rebellion: A Compilation of the Official Records of the Union and Confederate Armies.* Washington: Government Printing Office, 1880-1901.

State

Acts of the Seventh Biennial Session of the General Assembly of Alabama 1859-60. Montgomery: Shorter and Reid State Printers, 1860.

Acts of the Called Session of the General Assembly of the State of Alabama, January 1861. Montgomery: Shorter and Reid State Printers, 1861.

Acts of the Second Called Session 1861 and of the First Regular Annual Session of the General Assembly of Alabama. Montgomery: Montgomery *Advertiser* Book and Job Office, 1862.

Acts of the Called Session 1862 and of the Second Regular Annual Session of the General Assembly of Alabama. Montgomery: Montgomery *Advertiser* Book and Job Office, 1862.

Acts of the Called Session 1863 and of the Third Regular Annual Session of the General Assembly of Alabama 1863. Montgomery: Saffold and Figures State Printers, 1864.

Acts of the Called Session 1864 and of the Fourth Regular Annual Session of the General Assembly of Alabama. Montgomery: Saffold and Figures State Printers, 1864.

Journal of the Seventh Biennial Session of the House of Representatives of Alabama. Session of 1859-1860. Montgomery: Shorter and Reid State Printers, 1860.

Journal of the Called Session of the House of Representatives of the State of Alabama Commencing January 14, 1861. Montgomery: Shorter and Reid State Printers, 1861.

Journal of the Second Called Session 1861 and the First Regular Annual Session of the House of Representatives of the State of Alabama 1861. Montgomery: Montgomery *Advertiser* Book and Job Office, 1862.

Journal of the Called Session 1862 and the Second Regular Annual Session of the House of Representatives of the State of Alabama 1862. Montgomery: Montgomery *Advertiser* Book and Job Office, 1863.

Journal of the Called Session 1863 and the Third Regular Annual Session of the House of Representatives of the State of Alabama 1863. Montgomery: Saffold and Figures State Printers, 1864.

Journal of the Seventh Biennial Session of the Senate of the State of Alabama: Session of 1859-1860. Montgomery: Shorter and Reid State Printers, 1860.

Journal of the Called Session of the Senate of the State of Alabama 1861. Montgomery: Shorter and Reid State Printers, 1861.

Journal of the Second Called Session 1861 and the First Regular Annual Session of the Senate of the State of Alabama 1861. Montgomery: Montgomery *Advertiser* Book and Job Office, 1862.

Journal of the Called Session 1862 and the Second Regular Annual Session of the Senate of the State of Alabama 1862. Montgomery: Montgomery *Advertiser* Book and Job Office, 1863.

Journal of the Called Session 1863 and the Third Regular Annual Session of the Senate of the State of Alabama 1863. Montgomery: Saffold and Figures State Printers, 1864.

Newspapers

All of the following bound volumes of newspapers at the State Department of Archives and History in Montgomery were used in the research for this monograph. The date of the first and last issue of the newspaper found in each volume is given, except in cases where only one or two issues of the newspaper were used.

Eufaula *Daily Times.* 11 May 1872.

Florence *Gazette.* 18 January 1860-25 December 1861.

Gainesville *Independent.* 2 October 1858-23 September 1865.

Greensboro *Alabama Beacon.* 6 January 1860-3 January 1862; 10 January 1862-29 July 1864; 13 January 1865-25 December 1869.

Grove Hill *Clarke County Journal.* 1 January 1863-28 December 1865.

Huntsville *Democrat.* 15 April 1861-24 July 1861.

Jacksonville *Republican.* 5 January 1860-20 December 1860; 21 December 1860-26 December 1861; 2 January 1862-25 December 1862; 1 January 1863-21 November 1863.

Memphis *Daily Appeal.* (Grenada and Jackson MS) 9 June 1862-11 May 1863; 6 June 1863-30 June 1864; 21 September 1864-30 March 1865; 8 September 1864-April 1864 (beginning 8 September 1864, published in Montgomery and bound with Montgomery *Daily Advertiser* and Montgomery *Daily Mail* [mixed]; 8 January 1864-5 December 1865.

Mobile *Advertiser and Register.* 5 June 1861-31 October 1861. On 2 June 1861 the *Register* combined with the Mobile *Daily Advertiser* to form the Mobile *Advertiser and Register.*

Mobile *Advertiser and Register,* 18 January 1862-28 December 1862; 1 January 1863-30 June 1863; 1 October 1863-31 May 1864.

Mobile *Daily Advertiser.* 1 December 1860-30 April 1861.

Mobile *Daily Register.* 1 February 1859-5 January 1860; 11 January 1860-2 June 1861.

Mobile *Tribune.* 8 July 1861.

Montgomery *Daily Advertiser* and Montgomery *Daily Mail* [mixed]. 5 December 1863-31 August 1864. Unlike the Mobile *Advertiser and Register,* the Montgomery *Advertiser* and *Mail* did not combine for the duration of the war, but they are often found bound together in that period.

Montgomery *Daily Advertiser.* 5 May 1864-14 August 1864.

Montgomery *Daily Advertiser* and Montgomery *Daily Mail* (mixed), 1 September 1864-19 June 1865.

Montgomery *Daily Mail.* 14 October 1862-26 July 1863; 2 January 1864-31 August 1864; 11 April 1865-3 December 1865.

Montgomery *Daily Post.* 1 January 1861-31 December 1861.

Montgomery *Weekly Advertiser.* 1 October 1862-30 September 1863; 7 October 1863-21 September 1864.

Montgomery *Weekly Confederation.* 1 January 1859-29 March 1860; 7 April 1860-16 August 1861.

Montgomery *Weekly Mail.* 10 May 1862-22 April 1863; 29 April 1863-26 April 1864.

Montgomery *Weekly Post.* 18 July 1860-17 July 1861.

Prattville *Autauga Citizen.* 3 January 1861-19 December 1861.

Selma *Morning Reporter.* 27 May 1864.

Southwestern Baptist. 5 May 1859-15 May 1862.

Troy *Southern Advertiser.* 7 December 1860-17 December 1867.

Tuscumbia *North Alabamian.* 21 December 1860.

Obituaries

Obituary of Andrew Barry Moore in Mobile *Daily Register,* 10 April 1873.

Obituary of John Gill Shorter in Montgomery *Advertiser,* 30 May 1872 and Mobile *Register,* 30 May 1872.

Obituary of Thomas Hill Watts in Mobile *Daily Register*, 17 September 1892 and Montgomery *Advertiser*, 17 September 1892.

SECONDARY SOURCES

Books

Amland, Curtis Arthur. *Federalism in the Southern Confederacy.* Washington: Public Affairs Press, 1966.

Armes, Ethel. *The Story of Coal and Iron in Alabama.* Birmingham: The Birmingham Chamber of Commerce, 1910.

Barney, William L. *The Secessionist Impulse: Alabama and Mississippi in 1860.* Princeton: Princeton University Press, 1974.

Bible and Publication Society. *The Death Bed of Ex-Governor John Gill Shorter.* Philadelphia: n.d.

Brantley, William H. *Banking in Alabama, 1815-1860.* 2 vols. Birmingham: Privately Printed, 1961 and 1967.

Brewer, Willis. *Alabama: Her History, Resources, War Record and Public Men.* Montgomery: Willo Publishing Co., 1872.

Cauthen, Charles E. *South Carolina Goes to War, 1860-1865.* Chapel Hill: University of North Carolina Press, 1950.

Coulter, E. Merton. *The Confederate States of America, 1861-1865.* Baton Rouge: Louisiana State University Press, 1950.

Denman, Clarence P. *The Secession Movement in Alabama.* Montgomery: Alabama State Department of Archives and History, 1933.

Dodd, Donald B., and Wynelle S. Dodd. *Winston: An Antebellum and Civil War History of a Hill County of North Alabama.* Vol. 4 of *Annals of Northwest Alabama.* Compiled by Carl Elliot. Birmingham: The Oxmoor Press, 1972.

Dorman, Lewy. *Party Politics in Alabama from 1850 through 1868.* Wetumpka AL: Wetumpka Printing Co., 1935.

Eaton, Clement. *A History of the Southern Confederacy.* New York: MacMillan, 1954.

Ellison, Rhoda Coleman. *History and Bibliography of Alabama Newspapers in the Nineteenth Century.* University AL: University of Alabama Press, 1954.

Escott, Paul D. *After Secession: Jefferson Davis and the Failure of Confederate Nationalism.* Baton Rouge: Louisiana State University Press, 1978.

Fleming, Walter L. *Civil War and Reconstruction in Alabama.* New York: Columbia University Press, 1905.

Garrett, William. *Reminiscences of Public Men in Alabama for Thirty Years.* Atlanta: Plantation Publishing Company Press, 1872.

Gates, Paul W. *Agriculture and the Civil War.* New York: Alfred A. Knopf, 1965.

Hoole, William Stanley. *Alabama Tories: The First Alabama Cavalry, U.S.A., 1862-1865.* Tuscaloosa AL: Confederate Publishing Company, 1960.

Jones, James Pickett. *Yankee Blitzkreig: Wilson's Raid through Alabama and Georgia.* Athens: University of Georgia Press, 1976.

Little, J. B. *The History of Butler County, Alabama.* Cincinnati: Elm Street Publishing Co., 1885.

Lonn, Ella. *Desertion during the Civil War.* New York: Century Company, 1928.

_____. *Foreigners in the Confederacy.* Chapel Hill: University of North Carolina Press, 1940.

_____. *Salt as a Factor in the Confederacy.* New York: Walter Neale, 1933.

McKitrick, Eric L. "Party Politics and the Union and Confederate War Efforts." In *The American Party Systems: Stages of Political Development.* Edited by William Nisbet Chambers and Walter Burnham. New York: Oxford University Press, 1967.

McMillan, Malcolm C., ed. *The Alabama Confederate Reader.* University AL: University of Alabama Press, 1963.

Martin, Bessie. *Desertion of Alabama Troops.* New York: AMS Press, 1932; reprint, 1966.

_____. *Desertion of Alabama Troops from the Confederate Army: A Study in Sectionalism.* New York: Columbia University Press, 1932.

Malone, Dumas, ed. *Dictionary of American Biography.* 20 vols. and index. New York: Charles Scribner's Sons, 1928-1937. Supplements 1-2, 1944-1958.

Moore, Albert Burton. *Conscription and Conflict in the Confederacy.* New York: Macmillan, 1924.

_____. *History of Alabama.* Tuscaloosa AL: Alabama Book Store, 1951.

Nichols, Roy R. *The Disruption of American Democracy.* New York: MacMillan, 1948.

Nuermberger, Ruth K. *The Clays of Alabama.* Lexington: University of Kentucky Press, 1958.

Owen, Thomas M. *History of Alabama and Dictionary of Alabama Biography.* 4 vols. Chicago: The S. J. Clarke Publishing Co., 1921.

Owsley, Frank L. *King Cotton Diplomacy: Foreign Relations of the Confederate States of America.* Chicago: University of Chicago Press, 1959.

_____. *State Rights in the Confederacy*. Chicago: University of Chicago Press, 1925.

Patrick, Rembert W. *Jefferson Davis and His Cabinet*. Baton Rouge: Louisiana State University Press, 1944.

Ramsdell, Charles W. *Behind the Lines in the Southern Confederacy*. Edited by Wendell H. Stephenson. Baton Rouge: Louisiana State University Press, 1944.

Representative Men of the South. Philadelphia: Charles Robson and Company, 1880.

Tatum, Georgia Lee. *Disloyalty in the Confederacy*. Chapel Hill: University of North Carolina Press, 1934.

Thomas, Emory M. *The Confederacy as a Revolutionary Experience*. Englewood Cliffs NJ: Prentice-Hall, 1971.

_____. *The Confederate Nation, 1861-1865*. In *New American Series*. Edited by Henry Steele Commager and Richard B. Morris. New York: Harper and Row, 1979.

Thornton, J. Mills III. *Politics and Power in a Slave Society: Alabama, 1800-1860*. Baton Rouge: Louisiana State University Press, 1978.

Vandiver, Frank E. *Ploughshares into Swords: Josiah Gorgas and Confederate Ordnance*. Austin: University of Texas Press, 1952.

Walker, Anne Kendrick. *Back Tracking in Barbour County*. Richmond: Dietz Press, 1941.

Wesley, Charles H. *The Collapse of the Confederacy*. Washington: Associated Publishers, 1937.

Yearns, Wilford B. *The Confederate Congress*. Athens: University of Georgia Press, 1960.

Articles

Alexander, Thomas B. ''Persistent Whiggery in Alabama and the Lower South, 1860-1867.'' *Alabama Review* 12 (January 1959): 35-52.

_____. ''Persistent Whiggery in the Confederate South, 1860-1867.'' *Journal of Southern History* 27 (1961): 305-29.

Atherton, Lewis E. ''The Problem of Credit Rating in the Ante-Bellum South.'' *Journal of Southern History* 12 (November 1946): 534-56.

Bailey, Hugh C. ''Disaffection in the Alabama Hill Country, 1861.'' *Civil War History* 4 (1958): 183-93.

_____. ''Disloyalty in Early Confederate Alabama.'' *Journal of Southern History* 23 (1957): 522-28.

Fleming, Walter L. "The Peace Movement in Alabama during the Civil War." *South Atlantic Quarterly* 2 (1903): 114-24 and 246-60.

Howard, Milo B. "Alabama State Currency, 1861-1865." *Alabama Historical Quarterly* 25 (Spring-Summer 1963): 70-81, 82.

Knapp, Virginia. "William Phineas Browne: Business Man and Pioneer Iron Operator." *Alabama Review* 3 (1950): 193-99.

Long, Durwood. "Unanimity and Disloyalty in Secessionist Alabama." *Civil War History* 11 (1965): 257-73.

Owsley, Frank L. "Defeatism in the Confederacy." *North Carolina Historical Review* 3 (1926): 446-56.

—————. "Local Defense and the Overthrow of the Confederacy." *Mississippi Valley Historical Review* 11 (1925) 490-525.

Ramsdell, Charles W. "The Control of Manufacturing by the Confederate Government." *Mississippi Valley Historical Review* 8 (1921): 231-49.

Scheiber, Harry N. "The Pay of Confederate Troops and Problems of Demoralization: A Case of Administrative Failure." *Civil War History* 15 (1964) 226-36.

Trexler, Harrison A. "The Opposition of Planters to the Employment of Slaves as Laborers by the Confederacy." *Mississippi Valley Historical Review* 27 (1940) 211-24.

Dissertations and Theses

Brannen, Ralph Neal. "John Gill Shorter: War Governor of Alabama, 1861-1863." Master's thesis, Auburn University, 1956.

LeGrand, Phyllis L. "Destitution and Relief of Indigent Soldiers' Families of Alabama during the Civil War." Master's thesis, Auburn University, 1964.

Lynch, Jeanne Hall. "Thomas H. Watts: War Governor of Alabama, 1863-1865." Master's thesis, Auburn University, 1957.

Robbins, John Browner. "Confederate Nationalism: Politics and Government in the Confederate South, 1861-1865." Ph.D. diss., Rice University, 1964.

Smith, Thomas Alton. "Mobilization of the Army in Alabama, 1859-1865." Master's thesis, Auburn University, 1953.

INDEX

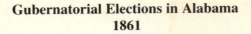

Gubernatorial Elections in Alabama
1861

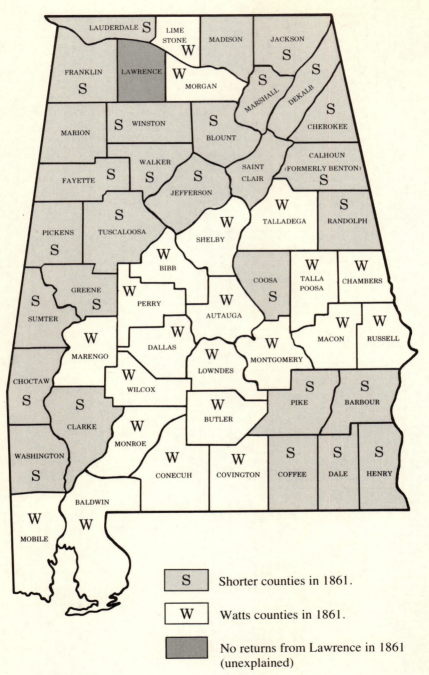

LAUDERDALE **S**

LIME STONE **W**

MADISON

JACKSON **S**

FRANKLIN **S**

LAWRENCE

MORGAN **W**

MARSHALL **S**

DEKALB

CHEROKEE **S**

MARION

WINSTON **S**

BLOUNT **S**

CALHOUN (FORMERLY BENTON) **S**

FAYETTE **S**

WALKER **S**

JEFFERSON **S**

SAINT CLAIR **W**

TALLADEGA **W**

RANDOLPH **S**

PICKENS **S**

TUSCALOOSA **S**

SHELBY **W**

COOSA **S**

TALLA POOSA **W**

CHAMBERS **W**

SUMTER **S**

GREENE **S**

PERRY **W**

BIBB **W**

AUTAUGA **W**

MACON **W**

RUSSELL **W**

MARENGO **W**

DALLAS **W**

LOWNDES **W**

MONTGOMERY **W**

CHOCTAW **S**

CLARKE **S**

WILCOX **W**

BUTLER **W**

PIKE **S**

BARBOUR **S**

WASHINGTON **S**

MONROE **W**

CONECUH **W**

COVINGTON **W**

COFFEE **S**

DALE **S**

HENRY **S**

BALDWIN

MOBILE **W**

W

S	Shorter counties in 1861.
W	Watts counties in 1861.
	No returns from Lawrence in 1861 (unexplained)